Within
the Circle

Within

★

th

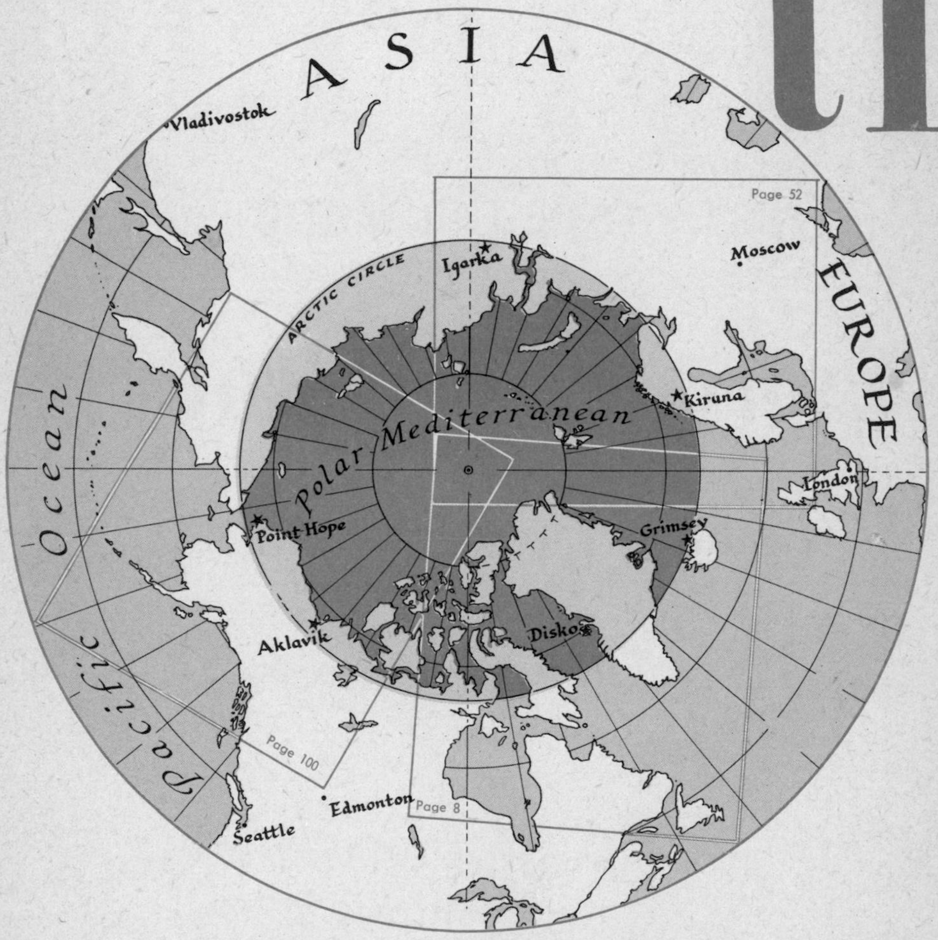

ASIA

Vladivostok

EUROPE

Page 52

Moscow

ARCTIC CIRCLE

Igarka

Kiruna

Ocean

Polar Mediterranean

London

Pacific

Point Hope

Grimsey

Aklavik

Disko

Page 100

Edmonton

Page 8

Seattle

★

CHARL

e Circle

PORTRAIT OF THE ARCTIC

By

Evelyn Stefansson

MAPS BY

Richard Edes Harrison

ILLUSTRATED WITH PHOTOGRAPHS

ES SCRIBNER'S SONS, NEW YORK

For my WASP sister, Julie, who one day will steer her plane northward to the lands within the Circle.

ACKNOWLEDGMENTS

A great many people helped make this book. Some generously lent unpublished material, others good naturedly submitted to long cross-examinations, and many lent photographs. Most thanks are owed Hugo Holten-Möller and Erling Porsild for help on the Disko Island chapter; Professor Halldor Hermannsson, Professor Steingrimur Arason and Consul General of Iceland in New York, Dr. Helgi Briem, for the Grimsey chapter; to Arnold Haverlee and Naboth Hedin for the Lapland and Kiruna chapters; to Dr. Ruth Gruber for the Igarka chapter; to Dr. Helge Larsen and Dr. Froelich Rainey for the Point Hope chapter; to Eliot Elisofon and *Life* Magazine for the Aklavik chapter and to Olive R. Wilcox for assistance with the whole. But most of all I am indebted to my husband, Vilhjalmur Stefansson, who patiently answered my innumerable questions with good humor, suggested improvements in the manuscript, and lent me his enthusiasm for the lands "within the Circle."

EVELYN STEFANSSON

Bethel, Vermont
August 19th 1944

Grateful acknowledgment is made for permission to use the following:

Photographs on pages 1, 9, 13, 36, 108, 114, 115, 116, 117 from the American Museum of Natural History.

Photographs on pages 57 through 61, 67 through 71, and 73 from the American Swedish News Exchange.

Photographs on pages 44, 45 from Oskar Bjarnason.

Photograph on page 131 and endpapers from Margaret Bourke-White, courtesy of *Life* Magazine.

Photographs on pages 129, 133, 135, 139 through 143, 147 through 155 from Eliot Elisofen, courtesy of *Life* Magazine.

Photograph on page 38 from Willard Fiske's "Chess in Iceland."

Photograph on page 27 from Jacob Gayer, courtesy of the National Geographic Society.

Photographs on pages 7, 16-17, 23, and 35 from Hugo Holten-Möller.

Photographs on pages 106, 107, 110, 111, 113, 121 from Dr. Helge Larsen.

Photographs on pages 101, 103, 105, 112 from Harold McCracken.

Photograph on page 40a from Porter McKeevor.

Photographs on pages 6, 20, 21, 25, and 26 from Erling Porsild.

Photographs on pages 122 through 126 from Dr. Froelich B. Rainey.

Photographs on pages 11, 43, 49r from Vigfus Sigurgeirsson.

Photographs on pages 74, 77, 78, 79 and 86 from the Soviet Embassy.

Photographs on pages 18, 19, 40b, 41, 46, 47, 49l and 50 from the U. S. Army Signal Corps.

Photograph on page 144 from A. Lincoln Washburn.

Photographs on pages VIII and 28 from Maynard O. Williams, courtesy of the National Geographic Society.

Photographs on pages 80, 81, 83 through 85, 89, 90, 193 and 95 from Sovfoto.

CONTENTS

Chapter I	NORTH TO EVERYWHERE	1
Chapter II	THIS IS GREENLAND	9
Chapter III	DISKO ISLAND: ICEBERG PAGEANT	21
Chapter IV	GRIMSEY: ARCTIC CHESS PARADISE	38
Chapter V	THIS IS LAPLAND	53
Chapter VI	KIRUNA AND GALLIVARE: ELECTRIC MIGHT IN THE LAND OF THE LAPPS	61
Chapter VII	THIS IS THE SOVIET FAR NORTH	74
Chapter VIII	IGARKA: SIBERIA'S BOOM TOWN	86
Chapter IX	THIS IS ALASKA	101
Chapter X	POINT HOPE: PREHISTORIC MYSTERY	108
Chapter XI	THIS IS CANADA'S NORTH	129
Chapter XII	AKLAVIK: DAIRY FARMING BY THE POLAR SEA	133
INDEX		157

Icebergs and the Alpine daisies on the opposite page are equally symbolic of the Arctic. The iceberg, a child of the glacier, is born when a huge piece breaks off, when the glacier "calves;" it may be several square miles in area and more than a thousand feet thick.

THE top of our world, fenced in by an imaginary Arctic Circle, is a strange and exciting wonderland. Once shrouded in a fog of superstition and folklore, it is emerging at last into the bright sunlight of our everyday world, to take its place importantly in the center of an overcrowded, expanding North Temperate Zone. Within the Arctic Circle lies a vast domain of prairies, lakes, forests, mountains and pack ice—this is to be the new crossroads of the world.

It is only forty years since the Wright Brothers invented the airplane, but how that discovery has changed our lives! Long-range planes are now busy changing the face of the world, shrinking its size, and making it round again. Of course we have known for centuries that the world was round, but we have been thinking and planning as if it were flat.

Here is proof. The newspapers tell us that many Army officers are flying home from Persia to New York by way of Iceland. Why in the world do they take such a roundabout route, we wonder. Get out your globe to plot the course and you will discover that it is the *shortest* possible way home. Find a piece of string to stretch from city to city and try again. This time between Washington, D. C., and the Philippines. About midway in your flight you are out in the Polar Sea directly over Wrangel Island, more than three hundred

1

miles north of the Arctic Circle and 100 miles north of northeastern Siberia. If you are surprised, you have been thinking of the world as flat. Experiment further and you will find that the shortest way between all the great capitals of the world, if they are far apart, is always North.

Three fourths of all the land in the world are north of the equator, and so are ninety per cent of the people who live in it. As the girth of the world decreases toward the North Pole, the distances between meridians of longitude narrow like the end sections of a peeled orange. If you have sixty or a hundred degrees of longitude to cover, you can fly it in less time, using fewer gallons of fuel, if you go northward in a great circle, or direct, route. Since this is the short way and the economical way, it is only a matter of time before our long range passenger and freight planes pattern the top of the world with a network of criss-crosses indicating their routes. "North to everywhere" will be the slogan of the air age.

It is not the lure of gold, copper and oil (all of which exist in large quantities in the Far North), but geography and long range planes that are rediscovering our long lost stepchild, the land of the midnight sun and midday moon.

If you were brought up to picture the world on a Mercator projection map, you would do well to wipe your mind's slate clean and start over again if you want a truthful picture of the Arctic. A Mercator map, you remember, is the one that treats the world as if it were a cylinder split up one side and spread out. It is invaluable for navigators charting a course, but worse than nothing for studying the Polar Regions, since it gives a distorted, completely erroneous impression. Greenland, for instance, appears to be about three times the size of Australia on such a map, when actually it is less than one third the size.

Imagine yourself flying *directly* from San Francisco to London. A Mercator map tells you to go a little north of eastward, passing through Missouri and Nova Scotia on your way. But consult a globe—you see the direct way is a little east of north, crossing the middle of Canada's Hudson Bay and Greenland's southern quarter. The globe is telling the truth, the Mercator map is not! The extent of its deception is shown on the opposite page by the portrait of a man which is drawn on a Mercator projection.

Since our earth is a sphere and our maps are flat, distortion is bound to occur somewhere. The trick, then, is in choosing the projection which least distorts the area you are interested in. A northern hemisphere projection like

On the left the man appears as he would according to the Mercator projection.

that on page .... gives a more accurate picture of the Artic Regions than any other.

In the center of the map is the Arctic "Ocean" which is not an ocean at all, but a real mediterranean sea, almost entirely surrounded by land. The word "ocean" is slowly disappearing from our maps and books and is being replaced with more appropriate terms like Polar Mediterranean, Arctic or Polar Sea, which were first suggested more than twenty years ago by Vilhjalmur Stefansson in his book *The Northward Course of Empire*. Too small for an ocean, the Polar Sea is really a large gulf off the Atlantic Ocean, which separates North America from Eurasia. Alaska, Canada and Greenland line the North American side, while opposite is the island group of Spitsbergen, then Lapland and the vast Soviet Arctic which comprises about forty-nine per cent of all the land border.

This is the Frozen Sea, the *Mer Glaciale,* as it was called in another era. What is it like? Two thirds of its surface is covered with pack ice, which is constantly in motion during all seasons of the year. The ice floes which make up the pack are of every shape and vary from the size of a piano or smaller, to fields several hundred square miles in area.

The larger ice floes make suitable landing fields for the biggest land planes. This was demonstrated when the Papanin Expedition of 1937 set up camp at the North Pole. Here they made about twenty different landings, some with heavily loaded planes, and each followed by a successful take off. In winter these strong level fields, each a potential emergency airport, are scattered throughout the whole of the Polar Sea. The water beneath them teems with many kinds of animal life from shrimps to seal, while above are polar bears, gulls and terns.

Icebergs, the children of glaciers, are never seen in the heart of the Arctic Sea, for they are born when the edge of a land glacier breaks off, or "calves." Spectacular in shape, they may be hundreds of feet thick, and several square miles in area. Except for Greenland and Northeast Land in Spitsbergen, there are few iceberg producing glaciers north of the the Arctic Circle. Therefore icebergs are rare on the Siberian coast, but many of these terrifyingly beautiful forms drift southward each spring to menace the North Atlantic shipping. One such berg was responsible for the "Titanic" disaster.

What kind of country surrounds the Polar Sea? Is it true that nothing grows there except a few stunted lichens and mosses? Are the only inhabitants a handful of Eskimos, fighting desperately for their lives against a harsh environment? What about the nights that are six months long? How much of what, as children, we learned about the Far North is true? How much false?

It took a war to bring the answers to many of these questions. Through the letters sent home by their GI fathers, brothers and sweethearts many people learned for the first time that Iceland was windy and rainy, but never very hot or very cold, and the "natives" living there were *not* Eskimos but a highly cultured people of Norwegian and Irish ancestry who had been in Iceland for more than a thousand years. They learned that winters at some of our Greenland bases were much warmer than those in Vermont. They heard of the wonderful crops that are raised in Alaska, and listened to complaints of how hot the summers were.

This book is not an attempt to paint the Arctic as a tropical paradise. It

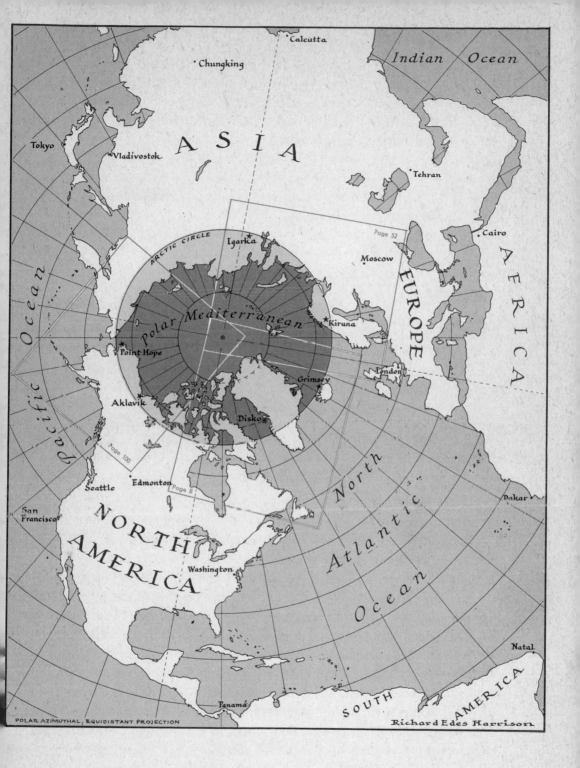

Indian Ocean

Calcutta

Chungking

Tokyo

ASIA

Vladivostok

Tehran

Cairo

Page 52

Igarka

Moscow

ARCTIC CIRCLE

Polar Mediterranean

Kiruna

EUROPE

AFRICA

Pacific Ocean

Point Hope

London

Aklavik

Grimsey

Disko

North

Page 100

Seattle

Edmonton

Page 8

San Francisco

NORTH

Atlantic

Dakar

AMERICA

Washington

Ocean

Natal

AMERICA

POLAR AZIMUTHAL, EQUIDISTANT PROJECTION

Panamá

SOUTH

Richard Edes Harrison

Icebergs off Greenland's rocky coast.

hopes to give a truthful glimpse of six widely separated and strikingly different communities which have in common a location north of the Circle.
These communities contain many kinds of people—Eskimos, Chukchis, Lapps
and Indians as well as Danes, Americans, Canadians, Russians and others.
These people are miners, scientists, doctors, missionaries, farmers, craftsmen,
hunters, trappers, schoolteachers, tradesmen and more. They lead variously
interesting and useful lives, most of them untroubled by the cold, the long
nights and other aspects of the Far North which are most terrifying to arm-
chair explorers. Their children play outdoors at 40° and 50° below zero, and
seldom miss a day of school, if there are schools in their neighborhood. They
grow up, marry, have children and die of accident, sickness and old age. Some
were born in the Arctic, as were their ancestors before them, but many have
migrated there, spurred by the eternal search for fortune, adventure, or a

better life. Their presence here seems to imply that they have found it.

This much at least is true. Without benefit of trickery or magic, a dairy farm operates almost at the shores of the Canadian Polar Sea at Aklavik, harvesting marvelously lush vegetable crops at the end of the comparatively short season. At the port of Igarka, in Arctic Siberia, where in pre-war days you could find ships from the ends of the earth loading virgin Siberian timber, a thriving, bustling town of twenty thousand has grown up within ten years. In Swedish Lapland are mountains of about the richest iron ore in the world, where miners, living in a model town, operate the completely electrified mine. Two hundred miles north of the Circle, at Disko Island in Greenland, people bathe in mountain lakes in summertime, and several varieties of orchids bloom. All this, and much more, lies north within the Circle.

Sled dogs love a nap in the snow.

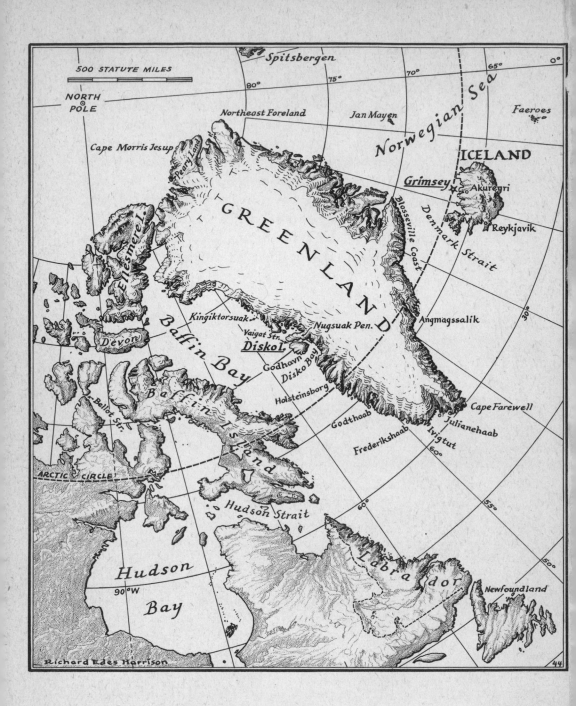

Most of us first learned about Greenland from the hymn that begins "From Greenland's icy mountains to India's coral strand," or the kindergarten classic that started: "Dear little Eskimo in his house of ice and snow," and ended: "for in Greenland there is nothing green to grow." Perhaps, then, it will come as a bit of a shock to learn that great stretches of the country are beautiful and green in summer and hundreds of varieties of flowers decorate its rolling hills.

Historically Greenland is the richest of all the American Arctic lands. It flourished as a republic for more than a hundred years longer than the United States has been in existence, at a time long before Columbus set sail on his voyage to the Indies.

"Largest of islands or smallest of continents," Greenland is the one Arctic country that nearly lives up to the old and popular conception of an ice-covered North. Unlike other lands surrounding the Polar Sea, most of Greenland's vast territory (726,000 square miles) is covered with a tremendously thick, permanently-frozen ice cover. This Inland Ice is the only true ice cap now remaining in the northern hemisphere, the one realistic memorial to the great ice sheets that used to cover much of North America, spreading as far south as New York and Iowa. The ice free fifteen per cent of Greenland

9

which lies on the coastal fringes adds up to an area more than equal to the whole of Great Britain, from Wales to Northern Scotland.

Most of Greenland is rugged, treeless, and essentially a country of grasses, sedges and small bushes. What the vegetation lacks in height it makes up in variety and more than four hundred and fifty varieties of flowering plants flourish throughout the land. In the more southerly parts birch trees may attain a height of thirty feet and willows eighteen feet. Even on Peary Land, the northernmost part of Greenland, summer finds butterflies and flowers bursting with color. On the Inland Ice, or Ice Cap, as the tremendous glacial mountain covering the interior of the island is sometimes called, some of the coldest temperatures in the world have been recorded, but on the marginal snow-free areas the winter climate resembles that of North Dakota and Wyoming, with many parts even milder.

Greenland is so long that her northern tip is the nearest land in the world to the North Pole, while her southern edge skirts the 60th parallel in the same latitude as Oslo and Leningrad. Her nearest neighbor, Canadian Ellesmere Island, lies only twelve miles to the northwestward and in wintertime you can cross the frozen strait that separates them in three hours if you walk briskly. Iceland, which is south of the Circle, lies one hundred and eighty miles from the east coast and may be seen in clear weather if you climb the mountains on the Blosseville Coast.

Almost a thousand years ago, in the year 981 to be exact, redhaired Erik Thorvaldsson was found guilty of manslaughter and outlawed from Iceland. Nick-named Erik the Red because of his fiery-colored hair, he decided to spend his three year exile exploring the unknown land seen many years before by one Gunnbjörn, when he was driven far off his course. Taking his family and Irish slaves, Erik sailed westward from Iceland and slowly skirted the southeastern shore of Greenland. Rounding Cape Farewell he landed on the beach at what is now the Julianehaab District. Here the party wintered while Erik explored the coast and matured plans for its colonization. With the canniness of a good real estate operator he decided that people would be more eager to colonize his new land if it had an attractive name, so he called it Green Land.

When his exile was over, Erik returned to Iceland with enthusiastic descriptions of his new land, and the next spring twenty-five ships set sail for Greenland. Some turned back and some were lost, but fourteen ships arrived and about three hundred and fifty settlers spent their first winter with no

Leif Eriksson, born in Iceland but a citizen of the Greenland Republic, discovered the North American mainland on his way home to Greenland from Norway. This towering statue of him was presented to the Icelandic people by the U. S. Congress in 1930, on the thousandth anniversary of Iceland's Parliament.

hardship or loss of life. Colonists continued to come until at one time there was an estimated population of nine thousand.

Five years after the first colonists arrived a parliament was established and Greenland became a republic.

Some years later Leif, son of Erik, on his way home to Greenland from Norway, made his history-making miscalculation. He took a course too far southward for Cape Farewell, or perhaps that southern extremity of Greenland was obscured by fog; at any rate he missed Greenland. Almost five hundred years before Columbus "discovered America" Leif Eriksson sighted a land he knew was not Greenland and stepped ashore on the mainland of North America. He named the new country Vinland, or Wineland, after the wineberries he found growing there. Knowing he had overshot his mark, Leif and his party turned northeastward and reached Greenland that summer where they told of their discovery.

In the fifteenth century trade relations between Norway and Greenland ceased and other sailings to Europe became few. There were scattered trading and whaling voyages no doubt, the traders coming chiefly from England, but we have no actual record of these sailings until Martin Frobisher in Queen Elizabeth's time. John Davis sailed up to Greenland a few years later and Davis Strait was named after him. Henry Hudson visited New York City, or at least the Hudson River, in 1607 and sailed up along the east coast of Greenland where now is Hudson Land.

About that time the Danes and Norwegians, who then had the same King, began to search for the Icelandic colonists in Greenland and they kept this up sporadically until 1721, when the Norwegian Hans Egede made the first permanent modern settlement in Greenland. He found ruins of homes and churches there but no people whom he recognized as Europeans. We know now that the men and women whom he mistook for pure-blooded Eskimos, because they spoke only Eskimo and lived only by hunting, were really mixed blood descendants of the European farmers and Eskimo hunters who had been joint occupants of Greenland in the historic period a few centuries earlier.

The eighteenth century found Greenland belonging to Denmark and the slow re-colonization of the country starting. Trading with the Eskimos began, whaling was successful, and before long explorers began to fill in the blank parts of the map. The long list of their names evokes pictures of romance and endurance, hardship and death. Baffin, Hall, the tragic Greely expedition, Fridtjof Nansen's crossing of the Inland Ice, Peary's dash for the

Young Eskimo mother and child from Peary's old winter quarters at Etah, the most northerly settlement in the western hemisphere.

Pole, the journeys of Rasmussen and MacMillan—to name only a few. Each helped in some measure to push back the frontiers of ignorance surrounding this strange land.

Today, while less developed commercially than the other Arctic countries, Greenland's social progress stands far above that of Canada and Alaska. To protect its seventeen thousand Eskimos from disease and liquor, the Danish Government has kept the country "closed" to all foreigners, even the Danes. Besides the Eskimos, or Greenlanders, there are about five hundred Danes holding administrative positions, and about a dozen Norwegians, comprising the total population of the huge island.

No foreign ship may seek harbor in Greenland except in the case of a dire emergency, such as engine trouble, or the lack of water. Several special harbors may be entered by foreign as well as Danish ships on condition that strict hygienic rules are observed. No commercial companies, Danish or otherwise, have been allowed to establish relations with the Eskimos. Only scientists, a very few artists and occasional visitors are allowed to set foot on Greenland soil and even they must first obtain the consent, formerly of the

Greenland Administration in Copenhagen, but temporarily since the invasion of Denmark, from the Danish Consulate-General in New York. Entrance permits are granted sparingly and only for excellent reasons.

The Danish Government, reserving for itself all trade with the Greenlanders, purchases the native products and fixes the prices to be paid. Five sixths of the price goes to the seller and one sixth to the Greenland Public Fund for use in public works, charity and emergencies. Articles considered necessities are sold at a very small profit, even at a loss, while luxuries such as tobacco and coffee, are higher priced although often hardly high enough to cover the original cost plus the high transport charges.

Liquor importation is strictly forbidden except in very small quantities for the use of the Danes. At Angmagssalik coffee and bread were also prohibited to prevent the Eskimos from getting used to luxuries which are difficult to obtain and which they can ill afford. While kerosene is sold everywhere, gasoline is considered too dangerous for the Eskimos to handle and its sale is forbidden.

Everyone in Greenland receives free medical care, free hospitalization and free medicines. All physicians are paid a fixed salary by the state and each district has a hospital at its main settlement with a resident Danish doctor and Danish nurse. At least once a year the doctor visits all the outlying settlements and outposts of his district in a motorboat provided for the purpose, which also serves as an ambulance for patients requiring hospital care.

Greenlanders are comparatively free from diseases which the Eskimos in Canada and Alaska have developed with the adoption of white man's food. Rickets and other deficiency diseases have made little headway here, one reason being that the government encourages the people to retain their old eating habits and sells them only small quantities of white man's food. The careful medical supervision and the government policy which keeps the country "closed" have resulted in the steady increase of Greenland's Eskimo population while that of Canada and Alaska has declined for years and is only just beginning to rise again.

The west coast of Greenland is divided into two inspectorates, the northern having its capital at Godhavn on Disko Island, the southern at Godthaab. The dividing line is at about 67° 30′ N. There are only two real settlements on the east coast and so there is no formal government there, but the heads of the trading stations act as representatives of the Greenland Administration.

At Ivigtut on the west coast is the only place in the world so far known where cryolite, an ingredient used in the manufacture of aluminum, is found in quantities large enough for commercial exploitation. This is Greenland's principal source of revenue and has yielded the Danish Government more than $15,000,000 in taxes. Oil, rendered from blubber, has been a chief article of export, as well as salted fish, and fox, walrus and seal skins. Eider down, feathers and mutton complete the exports·

Hunting, sealing and fishing are the three main occupations of the Greenlanders. The Government has so encouraged the raising of sheep that by 1935 there were already seven thousand of the animals divided between two hundred farmers on the southwestern coast.

On April 9, 1941, the first anniversary of the German invasion of Denmark, an agreement was signed between the United States and the Danish Minister, Henrik de Kauffmann, "on behalf of the King of Denmark" giving the United States the right to establish air bases and other military and naval facilities in Greenland. The Greenland Delegation, set up soon after the Nazi occupation, has now been incorporated into the Danish Consulate-General in New York under the title of Danish Consulate-General—Greenland Section, and Minister de Kauffmann is now looked upon by the American Government as "the spokesman for all Danish interests, including Greenland." Thus a new bond has been formed between our countries which is further strengthened by our soldiers now stationed in this land of greenness and glaciers. When the war is won and Denmark is again able to exercise sovereignty over her colony, the friendship and understanding born of our wartime relationship will continue to expand, increasing our interest in this vast and little known country.

Safe from the winds and icebergs outside, ships anchor in Godhavn's snug inner harbor, the finest in West Greenland.

These two aerial views show typical Greenland terrain of mountains rising steeply and magnificently from the shores of narrow, winding fjords. The bottom picture is from Ivigtut in southern West Greenland, the top one from much farther north.

The garden of the manager's house at the sheep station, Julianehaab.

Cultivated meadows at Julianehaab.

White-bearded Dr. Porsild, surrounded by his beloved plants and books, watches the icebergs parade past. The view on the opposite page was taken from his study window.

ICEBERG PAGEANT

THERE is a little house of science on a big island that lies off the middle of Greenland's incredibly long, and much indented, west coast. The island, named Disko, looks remote and out of the way on a map, and yet scientists from almost every corner of the globe have journeyed here to work, and to pay their respects to a kindly-faced, white-bearded scholar who presides over the birthplace and home of Greenland learning.

From his glassed-in study with its books, papers and potted plants, the seventy-three-year-old founder and director of the Arctic Station watches the continuous procession of icebergs parade slowly by, singly or in banks several deep, their beautiful forms resembling moulded ices specially designed for some gigantic celebration. He also watches another procession, the entire pageant of Disko life in which he takes an important part and much of which revolves around him.

The Eskimos tell a charming legend about an island that lay off a prosperous village of southern Greenland. They say that "once upon a time," or its

Eskimo equivalent, there dwelt in the village a mighty hunter who was also a powerful sorcerer. Each day as he went to hunt polar bear or seal he had to walk around the island to reach the sea, which lengthened his trip considerably. He grew tired of that and decided to tow the island away, which was not difficult, for he possessed great magical powers. He pulled a hair from his head, attached one end of it to the island and the other to his long, narrow, skin-covered kayak, and headed northward.

The magician paddled with all his strength and moved swiftly north along the coast until he was almost halfway up Greenland's western shore. He was passing Nugsuak Peninsula when an old woman who was a rival magician spied him. She laughed aloud to see him puffing so hard at what should have been an easy tow—the island is only about seventy miles long, sixty-five miles wide, and with only a few mountains on it more than six thousand feet high. Her ridicule broke the charm, the hair parted and the island settled to rest in its present position. As proof the story is true, Disko retains to this day its southern climate and vegetation.

At any rate, Disko needs explaining. It contains warm springs as well as glaciers, orchids as well as Arctic lichens, as though nature had accidently misplaced some southerly island two hundred miles north of the Arctic Circle!

Besides its exciting natural phenomena, Disko has a long and colorful history which began more than four hundred years before Columbus was born.

When the Icelanders colonized Greenland's west coast, at the end of the tenth century, a number of farmers settled in the region we know today as Godthaab, which is considerably south of Disko. In hunting, however, they penetrated far to the northward and often reached our island, which they called Bjarney, or Bear Island. Indeed, they hunted even farther north and sometimes spent the winter. This northern sojourn was such a common practice that the colonists had a special word for it, *nordurseta,* "north-dwelling."

It was from Bear Island that the first colonizing expedition to the North American mainland set sail. Thorfinn Karlsefni, with one hundred and sixty people and three ships, sailed in 1003 for the land first sighted three years before by Leif Eriksson. Three landings were made in the new country, at Helluland, Markland and Vinland, meaning respectively Flagstoneland, Forestland and Wineland. After three years, the expedition finally returned to Greenland chiefly because of various encounters with natives in which

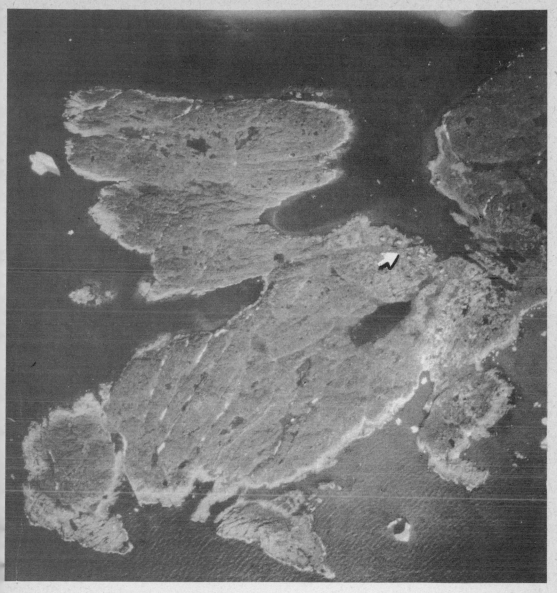

Southern Disko Island from the air. Godhavn is indicated by arrow.

many on both sides were killed. But not before a son had been born to one of the colonists. A great many present day Icelanders, most of whom are avid genealogists, are able to trace their ancestry back to this Snorri, the first white child born on the North American mainland.

From that time to this, much time and effort has been spent by scholars trying to locate exactly the three landfalls of the expedition. No one has indisputable proof, for the preserved narrative of the journey is too vague, but Helluland was probably Baffin Island, Markland southern Labrador, and Vinland somewhere in the vicinity of the Gulf of St. Lawrence, around Nova Scotia, New Brunswick and northern Maine.

As we have said, the European colonists of Greenland hunted much farther north than Disko. We know this because about 1333, three hunters spent a winter on the rocky little island of Kingiktorsuak, about 200 miles north of Disko, and very considerately left us a record of their stay. They built three beacons, or cairns, which were discovered nearly five hundred years later, and among the ruins of one was found a small slate stone bearing a runic inscription which reads: *Erling Sigvatsson and Bjarne Thordsson and Enridi Oddsson on the Saturday before Gangdag (April 24) made this (these) cairns.* From the style of the runes and the language, experts are able to date them fairly accurately. This is the farthest north that mediaeval Europeans have been traced beyond dispute, but there is little doubt among students of this fascinating period that they hunted and eventually settled down to live much nearer the Pole.

Timber, for housebuilding and other uses, was of great importance to these early colonists. As in Iceland, which is also treeless, wood had to be imported, much of it from Norway. Voyages for timber were also made to Labrador and perhaps to Newfoundland. The precious driftwood was also gathered along the shores of the settlement and on long summer journeys made especially for the purpose. Then as now, most wood came ashore between 61° and 68° N, making the region around and south of Disko a favorite place for gathering driftwood.

As one approaches Disko Island from the south, the dark, snow-capped island gradually takes form. Slowly the details become sharper, valleys appear, and one can see that the eastern part of the island has gentler slopes and more undulating forms than the rest of the island. The mountains are not as high nor as spectacular as some on the nearby mainland, because they are basaltic table mountains, and there are no peaks. This makes it difficult to determine from a distance which parts are highest. Above three thousand feet most of the ground is covered by highland ice, a distinction from Inland Ice, a term reserved for the great ice cap of Greenland.

The Greenlanders call Disko Kekertarssuak, the Big Island. It is a big island, a good deal larger than Rhode Island or Delaware and almost as large as Connecticut. Roughly triangular in shape, it shows its western face to

(*above*) Disko's flat-topped basalt mountains are a contrast to the usual sharp Greenland peaks. (*below*) The Danish Arctic Station, Disko.

Baffin Bay, and three deep fjords indent this side of the island. Vaigat, a narrow strait, separates its northeastern side from Greenland proper, and along the southern shore deep valleys extend from coast to coast or run far inland to be hidden by the glaciers. A large bay, which takes its name from the island, fills the gap between Disko and the mainland.

No volcanoes now disturb Disko with their troubled rumblings, but this was not always so. Traces of former unrest have not entirely disappeared; there are signs of them still in the great number of warm springs which are really faint after-effects of a once-tempestuous activity. The waters of these springs are remarkably pure and supply Godhavn, Disko's main settlement, with the finest drinking water in Greenland, both winter and summer.

Because the volcanic activity of the basalt region is so comparatively recent, Disko is unparalleled in Greenland for the thermal springs it contains. Scattered over a large part of the island, they are particularly numerous on the south coast and in the interior of Disko Fjord, the most southerly of the three fjords which indent the western shore of the island. In several places the warm springs have created miniature oases, where southerly plants grow and prosper.

While the temperature of the springs is very moderate, ranging usually between 36° and 43° F., rarely attaining 65° F., it is nevertheless sufficient to prevent solid ice from forming off the coasts near the outflow of the larger springs.

In winter, snow drifts down from the mountains of Disko and covers the open springs. The warm air above them slowly thaws out vaulted caves where even in midwinter flies buzz and snails are active. If you break a hole in the roof of one of these caverns, the steam pours out into the frigid air as if from a miniature "volcano" or fumarole.

The fjords which open to Disko Bay freeze over by the middle of December, but the bay itself and the Vaigat are ice-filled only from the beginning of January until April or May. Sometimes it happens that the western ice of Baffin Bay is driven toward land. Then Disko Bay, instead of freezing from the shore outwards, as most bays do, freezes over from the outside inwards.

When this happens, great shoals of white whale and narwhal are often cut off from freedom in the still open part of Baffin Bay and are gradually crowded toward the head of Disko Bay. As the freezing continues and the

Most Greenlanders now have some European blood. This Godhavn belle seems to have little Eskimo blood.

Encased in a waterproof, hooded coat lashed to the small opening of his boat, the kayaker can turn somersaults again and again without getting himself or the inside of his boat wet.

area of open water slowly diminishes, the mammals are finally restricted to the dwindling open spaces in the ice from which they cannot escape unless the weather changes and the ice is broken.

Now, should the temperature fall as cold as —20° or —25°, wispy condensing vapors, formed by the comparatively warm water of the bay coming in contact with the cold air, rise from every tidal crack and pool of open water. Suppose a school of whales has been captured in one of these pools. Their warm breath will expand the thin cloud of vapor to a substantial column, visible for some distance, which announces their presence to any hunters who may be in the vicinity.

These crowdings of whales are known as *savssat*. When they occur, the Greenlanders from neighboring shores find extremely profitable hunting from the edge of the ice, with harpoon and rifle.

Caribou once abounded on Disko and formed part of the food supply of the islanders. More than a hundred years ago a great demand for skins resulted in reckless killing, which exterminated the animals entirely from the island.

There are still caribou on various parts of the mainland. The Greenlanders themselves have now formulated rules to conserve them, and other wild animals. The most important of the rules is that a hunter may shoot only such game as he can bring back himself. No longer may he shoot several caribou for their tongues, a choice delicacy, and leave the rest of the carcass, or shoot half a dozen for their skins alone. Few break these rules. If any do, they pay the heavy fines upon which they and their neighbors have agreed.

The only coal mine in Greenland is on Disko, at Kutdlisat, a town of about 800 on the northeastern shore. It supplies the needs of the entire west coast of Greenland, as well as some of the requirements of Danish ships which ply these waters. While it is not a good steam coal, it is excellent for domestic heating purposes, being more brittle, of a younger composition, and with a heating power estimated at only half that of good steam coal. It gives off less smoke than ordinary coal.

Greenlanders mine the coal from broad, horizontal seams in cliffs near the beach. There are no pit shafts; instead horizontal tunnels are cut into the hillside. The working conditions are ideal, for the temperature in winter inside the mine is around 8° or 10° below the freezing point, a good level for hard work. The coal is non-bituminous, so there are no troubles with gas, nor is there much dust and there is little danger from explosion.

At the southernmost point of Disko Island, nestling at the foot of high basalt cliffs that rise two thousand feet, is Godhavn, capital of North Greenland, known to the English whalers as Lievely. Since the romantic seventeenth century days of Baffin Bay whaling, when it was a most important port of call, many a mariner has watched breathlessly for the high, flat-topped cliff immediately northward of the port which would proclaim that his ship was about to reach safety in one of the best harbors in West Greenland. This snug retreat is sheltered from drifting ice and from the fierce southwestern storms that sweep the coast. Past the harbor, icebergs file by in dignified splendor and Greenlanders sit at their windows to watch the processions.

The steep rocky land that protects Godhavn, the most visited port in West Greenland, is cut by two deep gorges near the village. Down one of them flows Red River. After the first snowfall its ice-covered stream and its valley offer a good sledging route to the interior of the island and across to Disko Fjord.

A little more than half a century ago the famous Swedish-Finnish geologist, Nordenskjöld, found large blocks of pure nickel-iron near Godhavn and thought they were meteorites, those twisted, fallen remnants of shooting stars. But a later explorer, Steenstrup, proved that the iron, one block of which weighed 25 tons, came from the earth instead of from the sky.

It was not strange that Nordenskjöld thought that these masses of iron ore were meteorites, for some of the greatest ones in the world have been found in Greenland. Ross, in the early nineteenth century, was the first explorer to mention seeing them; but it remained for our own Admiral Peary, in 1895, to transport three huge, pock-marked iron masses to New York, where they may be seen today, at the American Museum of Natural History. One of these meteorites weighs thirty-six and a half tons, so you can see what a tremendous transporting job it was.

Many years after Peary, the well-known Eskimo-Danish ethnologist and explorer, Knud Rasmussen, discovered a fourth meteorite. A special expedition was dispatched to bring it to Copenhagen.

Eskimo houses were formerly built of rocks and sod, but now the dwellings at Godhavn, and at most other towns, are built of lumber which, in peace time, came from Denmark; during the war it comes from the United States. The average house is one and a half storeys and has a steep, peaked roof covered with tar paper. The Danish Government, through its Greenland Administration, provides coal for heating purposes at a low price. The government lends money without interest to build a home, material for which they also supply at low prices. Often it takes ten or twenty years for the Greenlander to pay it all back, but an exceptionally good fishing season may allow him to wipe out his debt in a single year.

Naturally enough, the grandest home in all Godhavn, a town of 300, belongs to the Governor of North Greenland, and is two storeys high and surrounded by a large fenced garden. A flagpole and a battery are in the foreground, the guns ready and waiting to salute any important personage who comes a-visiting.

The North Greenland archives are housed in a stone building, to protect them from fire, and are a gold mine of exciting historical documents that go back to the earliest days. If some historian "discovers" this material, he will find rich pickings.

Not far from the archives building is the village church, appropriately built in Old Norse style. It seats about two hundred and is well-filled each Sunday.

An old Danish whaling ship plies the waters of Greenland's west coast. When a whale is taken, it is brought to the nearest sizeable Eskimo settlement, often Godhavn, to be cut up. When the ship is sighted, towing its catch, there is great excitement in the little town; for the Eskimos receive the lean meat of the whale in exchange for stripping the blubber, and a time of feasting and holiday follows.

There is going to be plenty for all, but the work has to come first. Every person takes some part in the flensing, which is the technical word for skinning and cutting up a blubber animal, a seal, walrus or whale; each man and woman, boy and girl, confidently goes to his post at the right instant, as in a well-timed musical show.

Tools are sharpened and prepared. Half a dozen or so butchers, with razor-sharp spears, climb aboard the whale's back, and operations start. With deft strokes and little waste motion they dissect the great body from tail to head, cutting the blubber into squares, each piece with a slit into which is inserted a grappling hook. The chunks are dragged up the rocks to long wooden tables specially set up for the purpose, where the women salt the blubber and pack it into barrels for shipment, in peace time, to Denmark. This oil is likely to go into the making of Danish margarine, the most popular and highest priced of butter substitutes. A bucket brigade carries off as much blood as can be used for cooking; the surplus slowly reddens the water along the beach.

When at last the blubber has been removed the red meat is cut off and stacked on the rocks. Everyone chews *maktak,* a great Eskimo delicacy which consists of a square of raw whale skin with a layer of blubber attached. It has been variously described as having a peanut, walnut and even a mushroom flavor. At any rate the Eskimos, and some whites, adore it.

Whaling time means holiday time to the Greenlanders, and they also celebrate Christmas, New Years Day, Whitsun and Easter. But the holidays they look forward to with keenest anticipation are the birthdays of the King and Queen. On the King's birthday, the 26th of September, all the Greenlanders throughout the country receive *Kongekost,* or King's board. This gift of food usually consisting of raisins, coffee and pilot bread or other biscuit, naturally enough makes for a gay celebration. The Queen's birthday happily falls on the 24th of December, Christmas Eve, thus providing the wherewithal for a double celebration.

Since 1913 a journal printed in the Eskimo language has published twelve monthly issues each year in Godhavn. *Avangnamioq,* the Northlander, it is called. It is distributed throughout North Greenland as soon as it is off the press. It is sent in yearly volumes to the rest of the country from its printing plant, which is now housed in the town hall, the House of Assembly.

A mile westward of the town is the famous Arctic Station which for more than thirty years has been lovingly directed by its founder, Dr. Morten Pedersen Porsild. Here have gathered, at one time and another since its beginning, explorers and scientists of almost every nationality; here many a tenderfoot has acquired the necessary knowledge, technique and confidence to complete some exacting piece of scientific research. He has found encouragement, companionship, wise counsel.

Porsild first stepped ashore on Greenland in 1898, as a young botanist. On his return to Denmark from his first expedition, he conceived the idea of establishing a northern laboratory for experimental research in every branch of science. His dream did not come true until seven years later. Then, through the generosity of a public spirited citizen, Porsild was enabled to return to Greenland and the Arctic Station began to take shape. It soon proved its worth and not long afterwards the Danish Government took over its care. Each year, until the invasion of Denmark by Germany, the government appropriated money for its maintenance and activities.

While not large, the station is well designed, well built and well equipped. Its most important function, of course, is to provide working space for scientists engaged in original research; but it provides living quarters as well for its director and four visiting scientists.

Dr. Porsild, although primarily a botanist, is acknowledged to be the leading authority on both the natural history of Greenland and its Eskimo culture. Through the years the scope of his interest has broadened, to include geology, glaciology and meteorology. His station has been the life and soul of every kind of scientific survey of Greenland, and serves as a base from which the geographical, geological, botanical and physical investigation of the land continues steadily. Its Arctic library, swelled by contributions from Danish and foreign societies, now contains fifteen thousand volumes; its herbarium contains more than fifty thousand specimens of plants. There is a meteorological station and a completely equipped small observatory, with two seismographs for recording earthquakes.

One activity of this miniature Hall of Science is training, in the special techniques of polar travel and investigation, young scientists who want to make a career in Arctic exploration and research. This explorer's apprenticeship has no doubt saved numerous lives; it has helped to provide secure foundations for reputations earned in various fields. Archaeologists learn here about the special problems connected with excavating specimens from frozen sub-soil. An ethnologist gets a chance to try out his book knowledge of Pidgin Eskimo; a botanist has Porsild's rich store of experience to draw upon for knowledge and inspiration.

When foreign scientists come to Greenland the station's chemical laboratories, thermometers, barometers, balances and equipment for field journeys are usually put at their disposal. They may also use the darkroom and its photographic equipment.

The choice of Godhavn as a base for scientific work was particularly fortunate, for several reasons. To begin with, the period of open water is comparatively long, so that ships can get here from other countries during more months than usual for a Greenland port so far north. The warm springs produce luxuriant vegetation, making this a botanist's paradise.

Dr. Porsild's first love has always been botany. His two monumental volumes, "The Flora of Greenland" and "The Seed and Reproduction of Arctic Plants," are nearing completion.

Nearly all botanists who have hunted plants in Greenland have stopped at Porsild's station to pay their respects and compare notes. With the collaboration of his two sons, Thorbjörn and Erling, innumerable botanical trips have been made to swell the herbarium. Porsild senior has discovered many new species of plants; each of his sons has found new species also.

Erling, the younger son, a well-known botanist in his own right, is a curator of the National Museum in Ottawa. Now a Canadian, he has recently been appointed Consul to Greenland and so divides his time between the two posts. He is peculiarly well qualified for his new position since he speaks Eskimo, Danish and English with equal facility.

Most travelers, coming to the Arctic for the first time, are astonished at the variety, color and abundance of Arctic vegetation; for the misleading statement "in Greenland there is nothing green to grow" was learned and believed by generations of our school children.

Some of the plants at Disko are useful as well as decorative. One of the most characteristic flowers, Arctic heather with its dainty, cream-colored bell blossoms, is used for fuel. Collected in large quantities by the Greenlanders, it burns well even when it is wet because of its highly resinous quality. Certain types of willow also make excellent fuel. The bushes are pulled up in summer, stacked to dry, and burned in the wintertime.

Some plants provide heat; others, like Archangelica, are a source of food. This is the largest and most conspicuous herb in Greenland, and its young stems and leaf stalks are eaten by the Eskimos who make long journeys to gather it.

Willows are found here, but they are not the willows we know. The tallest grow only waist high in Disko, although they are twenty and even thirty feet high in southern Greenland. Some of the trunks of the Disko trees are not thicker than a man's thumb, although they may be fifty or more years old. But, as with the largest California redwood, their age can be determined by counting the rings of growth. Rising slightly higher than the trees themselves, are their soft, fuzzy catkins, round which the bumblebees buzz.

There is a kind of willow "tree," that might easily have come out of Gulliver's Travels in Lilliput, for it rarely grows more than one inch high, and each summer bears only a few little leaves and tiny catkins. This is

The midnight sun gleams through the clouds and is reflected a thousand-fold by the snow.

Poppies, one of the commonest Arctic flowers, line the shores of many Greenland fjords.

probably the smallest tree in the world. It is found on Disko in the outlets of the warm springs and in the moist, boggy spots of the island.

On the purely decorative side, white, star-like little mountain avens, belonging to the rose family, often color a whole mountain side with their abundant blossoms. Arnica alpina, a bright yellow flower resembling a miniature Kansas sunflower, rhododendron, chickweed, and six or more varieties of saxifrage also grace the landscape. The most beautiful of the latter family is the purple variety; their gorgeous blooms are first in spring and can sometimes be seen bordering the snowdrifts.

Plumy cotton grass waves its white tassels along river banks and pools; rare mosses, and several kinds of fern, grow profusely in the earth between the stones of the rock ledges. Lovely little pink, bell-shaped flowers, as delicate as lilies of the valley, are borne by two members of the cranberry clan. Last, but far from least, *five* species of the orchid family reproduce themselves and flower perfectly. One explorer tells that two varieties grow in such profusion along the narrow flats of the Disko shore that in walking over them one crushed so many blossoms that the air was made sweet with their perfume.

Dr. Porsild, despite his age, still continues active. He usually works until four in the morning, rising each day at eleven. Despite his many scientific endeavors he finds time to take an active interest in political matters and is constantly championing causes for the Greenlanders. He holds the distinction of being the only non-Greenlander ever elected to the Parliament, where he represented the Greenlanders, not the Danes (of whom there are about a dozen at Godhavn).

In his sun-filled study, where he has a front row seat for the iceberg parade, Porsild continues his studies of glaciers, as well as their offspring the icebergs. Some of the bergs are born at the head of Disko Bay from mighty glaciers, others come from Melville Bay farther north. Most of them are being carried irresistibly southward, to fade away and die in the warm waters of the North Atlantic.

On their way out of the bay, groups of bergs are sometimes captured on the shallow bars east of Godhavn, where they are grounded. Here the sunshine and warm current break them into fragments, to the accompaniment of thunderous, warlike roars and crashes. As they crumble they set up waves that break high and fiercely upon the neighboring shores.

Every sound of Greenland, from the rending crashes of the toppling berg giants to the soft whisper of the farthest wave which they send out, is music and speech to the gracious scientist of Disko.

ARCTIC CHESS PARADISE

GRIMSEY is a tiny Arctic island, rising steep and lonely from the cool waters of the Polar Sea. Its claim to fame lies in the superior skill of its citizens at the most intellectual of all games, chess.

Some say that the rocky island, which lies twenty-five miles north of Iceland, was first settled almost a thousand years ago by outlaws, who found solace during the long winter nights in playing the intricate game. They played so often they became expert and handed the art down from generation to generation until Grimsey's fame spread throughout Iceland. History does not confirm this tale but there *has* been a tradition, reaching back to the middle ages, that those who dwelt on Grimsey were superlative chess players. To this day both in summer evenings, and when the harvest is in, and the shadow of winter reaches the island isolating it from the mainland, the simple farm and fisher folk who dwell there bring out the chess boards and the play begins.

Here is a typical story of polar chess in the middle ages. It is worth retelling because it is the kind of tale the Icelanders have been telling about Grimsey for hundreds of years, and because it comes from a fascinating book called *Chess in Iceland* by Willard Fiske; but of him—more later.

Long years ago, when the Bishop of Holar was one of Iceland's great dignitaries, a fourteen-year-old lad from Grimsey, whom we shall call Gisli (Gees-lih), since history does not record his name, accompanied his father on a visit to the episcopal seat. He had never before left his birthplace on the little isle and consequently, as with Phyllis in Gilbert and Sullivan's *Iolanthe,* his manners were "rustic but hearty." All were equal in Grimsey and he had never learned the special respect due persons of high degree.

While father and son mingled with the crowd in the court of the Bishop's house, the prelate himself passed through, and all doffed their caps, except Gisli. When reproved, he asked:

"Who then was that man?"

"The bishop, you fool, the highest priest in Iceland."

"Oh, the bishop—is he a good chess player?" Without waiting for a reply he answered his own question: "But of course he is, for our parson at Grimsey is the second best player on the island."

His remarks were carried to the bishop who sent for Gisli.

"What was it that you asked in the court?" he inquired.

"I only asked one of your people if you played a good game of chess," said Gisli, "for, if you do, I should like to try one with you."

Now it happened that not merely was the bishop an excellent chess player, he was also rather vain about his playing. Amused at the boldness of the country bumpkin, he ordered a chess board to be brought, and, to his astonishment, lost three straight games.

"Where did you learn your chess?" sourly asked the bishop, who was not taking his defeat too gracefully.

"From my father and his people in Grimsey, for in the winter we play from early in the morning until late at night."

"I rather suspect you learned it from the Devil, and that you have been neglecting your prayers," said the humiliated bishop.

"If that were true," said Gisli, "I should have no difficulty beating the Devil, for I can beat our parson who is a pious and holy man, and he can beat everybody else."

The bishop regained his humor at the lad's reply and finding him clever at other things as well as chess, he sent him to the cathedral school. Later he became a good and pious priest, and in those days no honor could be much greater than that in Iceland.

What kind of an island is this that has produced so many chess experts?

Grimsey is the one truly Arctic part of Iceland, which country lies south of the Circle except for a tiny strip of land on its northeastern coast. Only three miles long and half as wide, you can traverse Grimsey's entire shoreline in a two-hour walk. In summertime the sea which separates it from the mainland is calm and beautiful, transformed by the midnight sun into liquid gold. But in winter the stormy winds blow furiously, and frequent gales whip the waves so roughly and so high that the rocky foundations of the little island literally quiver. Then Grimsey, which means Grim's Island, is separated from the rest of the world, for the trip to the mainland becomes suicidal, and only the slender but comforting thread of radio keeps its isolation from being complete.

Grimsey is part of Iceland, a country which can trace its history back through a thousand years to its very beginning. A land without trees, where fierce volcanic heat and magnificent blue glaciers contrast in majestic beauty. A land whose waters are warmed by the gulf stream, tempering the climate which is rainy, but never very hot or very cold. Here a pagan people, developed a system of self-government and law, and invented trial by jury. Today Iceland boasts the oldest parliament in the world, which has functioned without a break for more than a thousand years. It is a land of poets with a rich heritage of sagas and eddas, which were recited and handed down by word of mouth long before they were written down.

There is no illiteracy in Iceland! The island is the most bookish in the world, reading and publishing many times more books per capita than any other country. At the remotest farm, or at the neighborhood barber shop you will find people who converse equally well on subjects ranging from classical history and Plato to the American Civil War and current world news.

The coasts of treeless little Grimsey are rocky, some rising steeply from the sea like the eastern shore, while the western is low and easily approached. From the coves on the latter shore the grass-grown land rises gradually to the inhabited part of the island and green patches of vegetation dot the black rock walls.

On the steep, eastern side of Grimsey every rocky cliff and shelf is inhabited by incredible numbers of every variety of sea bird. Each square inch of the greyish rocks is in use for perching or nesting, and the birds are so crowded that one rubs up against another with each movement. The air is filled with their noisy cries and as a boat approaches and sounds its horn, the birds fly off with a clatter so loud that conversation is impossible.

(*above*) This rocky shore of Grimsey looks as if some giant stone cutter had been at work neatly chipping sections away. (*below*) There are still some sod houses left in Iceland.

When peace is restored and the birds return to their perches, whitening the cliffs, the sea below becomes blanketed, too, with birds seeking their food in the water.

Both birds and eggs supply a substantial part of the islanders' food. The gathering of the eggs is a hazardous and fearful occupation, for the hunters must be lowered by a rope down the steep cliffs. Accidents occur, but not as often as you would think.

According to folk belief, the cause of these accidents was a troll or giant who lived in the cliff. As a man was being lowered, a hairy arm holding a long knife would appear suddenly, cut the rope and the man would fall to his death. The only known preventative was sprinkling with holy water and the singing of psalms.

In the thirteenth century there lived a courageous priest who determined to exorcise the evil spirit responsible for so many deaths. He had himself lowered down what was considered the most dangerous spot and instructed his parishioners to keep singing psalms, loudly and without pause, as long as he was below. This was to cover up the noise he would have to make, for he took with him under his priestly vestments a hammer. With this he broke away the sharpest and most dangerous rocky snags—the real cause of the trouble. This practical consecration of the cliff proved entirely successful and from that day to this the giant has not cut a single rope.

At the beginning of the tenth century, the waters round Grimsey were incredibly rich with seal, walrus and white whale. About this time the King of Norway sent a representative to Iceland who tried to secure a foothold on Grimsey—not exactly ownership, but something like the rights the United States has been given during World War II in connection with air bases abroad. Like many smaller nations today, the Icelanders wanted to be conciliatory; but they were deeply worried about possible extension of a foreign government's power once it was established on their soil. Parliament concluded that Grimsey was so rich in sources of food that if the Norwegian King had a right to station a fleet there, the fleet would be able to feed itself from the rich sea surrounding the island, and would then be capable of attacking the country, so permission was denied.

Today there is very little animal life most of the year in the sea around Grimsey, except that the fishing is excellent. But even now when northwesterly gales bring to the island the floes that ordinarily drift south along the east coast of Greenland, the ice brings with it a multitude of

Down the side of a cliff goes the egg-gatherer on a stout rope paid out in inches from above. His is a hazardous occupation.

Puffins nest on many of Grimsey's rock ledges. They and their eggs make good eating.

seals, and sometimes walrus and white whales. Even in recent years the chess-playing islanders have killed three or four hundred of these in a day.

But we know that there is not one sea mammal in the ocean for every ten there used to be, some think there is not one now for a hundred then. This is not strange, since from the reign of Queen Elizabeth to the development of kerosene a hundred years ago, most of the lamps of Britain and the rest of Europe were filled with the oil of whales, seals and walrus caught around Greenland, Iceland and Spitsbergen. Tens of thousands were slaughtered every year. Measured in gallons of blood, this is nearly or quite the bloodiest carnage we know from history.

Within the last hundred years, Grimsey changed from an island that was backward, in most things but chess, to one of Iceland's most progressive communities. This is saying a good deal, for Iceland has led many a larger country in her enlightened social reforms, managing the change from an almost mediaeval retarded country to a successful modern nation, practically abolishing poverty and providing the most adequate education and hospitalization for its people in the process.

The puffins are caught in flight with the long-handled net shown above.

Willard Fiske, a wealthy New England scholar who fell in love with Iceland during the second half of the last century, is credited by the Icelanders with much of Grimsey's progress. When Fiske, who was a famous chess-master, heard of Grimsey and its favorite recreation he almost adopted the little island. He became its devoted patron and sent chessmen and boards to the island at a time when they were very scarce. Although his interest in Grimsey lasted throughout his lifetime, Fiske never stepped foot on the island though he saw its profile in 1879 as he sailed by. He was deeply impressed that a community of less than a hundred, in money the poorest in all Iceland, should be so interested in chess and boast a much-read library of several hundred volumes.

When he died, this man, who was one of the first Americans to learn, master and love the Icelandic language and its literature, left part of his fortune in the form of a trust fund for Grimsey which did a great deal to improve its standard of living. It provided among many other benefactions

The annual round-up of Iceland's long-haired sheep is a sight people come from afar to see. These youngsters watch the final step—the sheep safe in the corral.

a library with a fund of about $100 a year for the purchase of new books. He could not have chosen a more appropriate gift, for next to chess the favorite pastime of the islanders is reading books.

On Grimsey, where the sun never leaves the sky in late June, the whole population lives on about fifteen farms, all of which are on the low, easily-approached western shore. One farm, standing off by itself, is the most northerly in all Iceland. Cultivated fields surround each farm, in most places meeting one another to form one continuous tilled area. Beyond the hedged-in hay fields are rich, grassy pasture lands. In spring small pools appear, most of which usually dry up by late summer. The island has several fountain-like springs emerging from the ground, which disappear during the long dry seasons. One pond survives most dry years.

Despite the scarcity of water during these very dry periods, the three or four hundred sheep on the island survive nicely. It has been noticed that they feed most vigorously at dawn and dusk when the grass is wet with dew and so absorb sufficient moisture for their needs, and many of them seem to go days without water. It is said that the number of ewes that have

The chief of the round-up is responsible for getting every last sheep from the hills into the corral.

twin lambs (some of them triplets!) is unusually large and that the four hundred sheep of late winter are six or seven hundred in summer, a number the Icelanders consider high for so small an island. Each fall nearly half of these are slaughtered for food.

The sheep on Grimsey have a coarse outer coat of wool which looks somewhat as if it were in overlapping layers designed to shed moisture, like shingles on a roof. In the heaviest rain the skins of the sheep remain dry. The outside or longer coat of guard hairs, called by the Icelanders *tog,* is removed separately and used for blanket making, while the inner and finer wool, the *thel,* is made into yarn intended for cloth. Most of the underwear, sweaters, mittens and socks worn by the islanders are knitted at home from wool that has been carded and spun for them by the mainland cooperatives. A few of the farms still have spinning wheels; carding, laborious when done by hand, is inexpensive and quick when done by machinery. So more and more wool is sent to the mainland for processing. The wool, which is woven into cloth, is either sewn at home or tailored into suits for the people by a cooperative tailoring establishment.

The islanders do not make their living by farming alone, for their lands are small. Few, if any, depend on fishing for their whole income. They usually combine fishing, the most important industry, with sheep-raising and egg-gathering. They are fairly self-sufficient, their twenty or thirty cattle producing plenty of milk, and the ocean providing tons of fresh fish. These foods are the staples; they are supplemented by homegrown potatoes and garden vegetables and by imported foods, purchased at the cooperative store. This store, incidentally, sells everything from food to farm machinery.

One of the chief reasons for the great advance of Grimsey this last hundred years, and one of the chief reasons for Iceland's success as a nation, is in the cooperative societies. The largest cooperative in the country has members from every level of the social ladder, from day laborers to supreme court justices. Icelandic cooperatives differ uniquely from those of other countries in that both the consumer and producer are united in a single society, thus eliminating the usual friction resulting from the difference in interest where buying, producing and selling cooperatives are kept separate.

An Icelandic cooperative society buys whatever goods are needed in a district, for consumption or manufacture, then sells them for cash if possible. In many cases, purchases are carried on the books until the products of the farmers and small fishing concerns are ready for market, which may mean an extension of credit from six months to a year. Forty-six of Iceland's cooperatives are combined in a federation, and one out of every nine Icelanders, including those on Grimsey, is a member of some cooperative. It is not necessary, of course, for more than one person in each family to be a member.

While gales are frequent and harsh in winter, snow does not worry the islanders, for the constant wind seldom allows it to settle. The sun never entirely disappears from Grimsey even during the shortest day in December, when there are at least three or four hours of light. No part of the island is more than five miles north of the Arctic Circle and you would have to be nearly a hundred miles farther north than that to lose the sun entirely at the time of shortest days.

School is compulsory for all children from the ages of seven to fourteen. Its one building houses the library endowed by Fiske. The community is too small to afford a teacher *and* a minister, so both are combined in one. This is a commonplace in small, remote Icelandic communities. Men destined for service in outlying districts must pass examination in both

48

Two typical young Icelanders. The girl on the right has gathered a bouquet of daisies which are called "Baldursbrá," meaning "The Brow of Baldur," one of the North European gods known to us chiefly from the Icelandic *Eddas*.

theology and education.

A large percentage of the island students go to the mainland for further education at high schools and colleges which are, like all schools in Iceland, free and run by the Government. The Government also supports the Church and you will never see a collection being taken. There is complete freedom of religion, and no compulsion to attend services. Many who are not church-goers listen regularly to the religious programs from the mainland broadcast on the radio.

There is one radio for every four or five persons in Iceland and most or all the farms of Grimsey have them. The broadcasting stations are government owned and no advertising is permitted except at one period during the day which is devoted exclusively to advertising, and this is during working hours when people are least likely to listen. A committee appointed by Parliament arranges the radio programs which include musical, recreational, religious and children's bedtime story hours. The programs usually most enjoyed and considered most important are those which present factual knowledge of both past and present, and the news of the day.

Some women still wear the national holiday costume on important occasions. The average farmer is well educated, extremely well read and loves to discuss obscure passages from the sagas.

The Government also runs the boat which carries Grimsey's people and their possessions back and forth to the mainland. Six scheduled trips are made each year and many unscheduled ones, especially in case of emergencies.

In earlier days, houses of turf were the fashion at Grimsey. These were superseded by wooden and corrugated iron houses, of the type common in the Alaskan and Canadian North. But now all new houses built on Grimsey are made entirely of reinforced concrete, in the most modern styles.

The reason why only beautiful modern houses are built is that when the Government lends a farmer money to build a house, it specifies that the design must be either drawn up by or approved by the Government architect. Large cities like Reykjavik have their own architects; the Government provides them for the smallest rural settlement. If a farmer is wealthy and does not need to borrow money, he may build any kind of house he wishes, and his plans need not be approved.

Scanning the records of Grimsey's life we find that the little island has survived terrible disasters, epidemics of smallpox and influenza, and many drownings. In the old days all traffic to and from the mainland was in open boats and sudden storms and windswept waves took frightful toll. One of many tragic episodes happened in 1793 when there was an epidemic in which so many died that, with the exception of the clergyman, there were only six able-bodied men left. These six tried to reach the mainland in a boat to seek help and were all drowned, and for some time the clergyman was the only grown man on the island to keep the women and children company. Several times the population has been decimated by drownings.

Strangely enough, the islanders have never become discouraged, and it seems to have been always true in the past as it is today that most of those born on the island stay there by choice. If they leave for any reason they usually come back, some of them in their old age. Those who nowadays move back to Grimsey have perhaps lived in the United States or Canada and have prospered. Some have lived in Reykjavik, the capital of Iceland, or in another of her cities. Some have studied and lived in Europe. But her wandering sons and daughters keep returning to the little isle from every part of the world. This is the place they long for if duty or circumstance prevents their going home—Grimsey with its peaceful, simple life, its birds and sheep, its books and its chess.

500 STATUTE MILES

NORTH ⊙ POLE

Cape Chelyuskin

Igarka

Yenisei

GREENLAND

Rudolf I.

Yenisei Gulf

Franz Josef Land

Kara Sea

Siberia

Northeast Foreland

Novaya Zemlya

Ob

S. R.

Spits-bergen

Barents Sea

Urals

Norwegian

Bear I.

Jan Mayen

Murmansk

Kola Pen.

U. S.

Sea

Lapland

White Sea

Archangel

ARCTIC CIRCLE

Kiruna

Volga

NORWAY

SWEDEN

FINLAND

Leningrad

Narvik
Luossavaara   Kiruna

Tornea

FINLAND

Trondheim

Helsinki

Malmberget
Gällivare

Oslo

Stockholm

Porjus

Baltic Sea

100 MILES

Lulea

SCOTLAND

Harrison

EAST of Greenland, west of Siberia, and fronting the Polar Mediterranean, is Lapland, a strip of northern Scandinavia, Finland, and a very small slice of the Russian part of the Soviet Union. It is neither a political nor even a geographical entity. It is simply those districts of northernmost Europe inhabited by Lapps, a happy-go-lucky, nomadic people whose culture revolves mainly about their herds of beautiful reindeer.

Each year the colorful Lapps journey into the mountains, following their deer to new feeding grounds. Reindeer are no respecters of man-made political boundaries and sometimes wander across the border between Sweden and Norway, but a special treaty between the countries sanctions these unorthodox border crossings. For the long trek into the mountains, camp gear and household goods are packed in boat-like sleds called *pulkas* or *akjus* which are drawn by reindeer. Old people and women ride in the sleds, while sturdy children alternately walk and run alongside the caravan, the red wool tassels of the boys' caps dancing gaily with each sudden movement. Youngsters too big for cradles take turns riding and walking, as the strong reindeer surefootedly pick their way over rocky terrain in single file.

53

The men tend the herds. They take turns at watching when the party stops at night to set up tents for food and rest. When the weather is fine all goes well, but sometimes on the return trip an early snow chills the young ones, who can no longer gaily shout and run alongside the *pulkas,* but have to be carried. Single reindeer stray from the herds and must be found; clothing becomes soaked and time must be taken to dry it.

About 30,000 of these Lapp folk are scattered north of the Arctic Circle. Where did they come from? There are too many answers—all theories.

The Lapps wear moccasins, somewhat like those of our North American Indians; many of their implements and customs are similar, leading many writers to link the origins of the two. Some writers have tried to prove that the old Chinese Imperial family was directly descended from the Lapps. But most scholars, especially those who have devoted decades to the study, have concluded that the threads of Lapp beginnings have become too tangled for unraveling. Who their nearest relatives are, and whence they came, seems likely to remain an unsolved mystery.

They are small of stature, these Lapps, the men commonly near four feet eight inches and the women four feet six. Their language, like Hungarian and Finnish, is related to that of the Eskimo with the difference that there are many Lapp dialects, while the Eskimos have remarkably few.

As a rule, Lappish faces are short and broad, with prominent cheek bones and with a wide mouth ready to break into a quick smile, for their sense of humor is good and a little thing will make them laugh. Their deep set eyes are of every color, blue, grey and brown; more often than not they have a Mongol slant. Outdoors life has trained them to notice small details at great distances. Their sight appears remarkably keen to an outsider, but this may be only because they know better than you what to look for and so notice things that would escape you. Their eyelids are often reddened, inflamed by camp fire smoke and the reflection of brilliant sunlight on snow.

Long ago these nomads ranged over vast tracts of northern Norway, Sweden, Finland and Russia, but as agriculture slowly pushed farther northward, they were confined to smaller and smaller areas, and today they are found chiefly in the northernmost and most mountainous regions. A few of them move away to cities and towns, or they become farmers and fishermen. Some have come to the United States and have had an average success similar to that of other European immigrants.

54

Surrounded by playmates, this Lapp boy sketches a young girl in her colorful costume.

The Lapps, or Samé as they call themselves, belong mainly in three groups. The wandering Mountain Lapps, much the largest group, follow their reindeer herds into the mountains and down again, endlessly on the move. The Forest Lapps live in the wooded districts, and their deer, stronger and bigger than those of the Mountain Lapps, graze among the low-lying forests and swamps. Their herds are much smaller than those of their nomadic brothers and have to be watched over continually lest they stray outside the boundaries of the grazing land into some neighboring farmer's meadow, for the owner must pay heavily for any damage. The last and smallest group are the Fisher Lapps who live mainly on the coast, or along the rivers and lakes.

Not so long ago the Swedish Government made an effort to "civilize" its Lapps. Many gave up their herds and tents and retired to real houses, to cultivate plots of land, to send their children to school, and cook on an iron

55

stove, a special joy to anyone who has had to keep a fire going with scanty, damp birchwood.

But with this comparative new-found ease there developed serious drawbacks. Many of their number, especially the children, contracted tuberculosis, and the use of alcohol was discovered, with the usual bad effect it seems to have on all primitive peoples. So now the Government has faced about and is encouraging return to the old way of life by framing new grazing laws, assuring favorable treatment for the Lapps in tax matters, and by purchasing a considerable number of reindeer each year which the state exports in the form of meat, antlers, leather and furs to various countries. Reindeer meat has been so popular in Stockholm that it has sold at prices somewhat higher than beef and mutton.

The Lapps, traversing the valleys and hills of four countries, have been little touched by our modern ways, and remain still a pastoral and nomadic people.

As a rule, Lappish faces are broad with prominent cheek bones, and wide mouths ready to break into a smile, for the Lapp sense of humor is good.

Tent folk of Sweden's Far North.

A Lapp and his coffee pot are seldom separated. Here a cup is brewed on the trail.

The Lapp's "kolte" or coat, is usually blue, with bright colored ribbons edging the seams.

The large red woolen tassel on his cap jumps and dances with every sudden move.

A Lapp child's costume is an exact replica of his parents' dress, with the addition of a pina-
fore in the case of this youngster. From childhood to old age Lapp women wear ruffle-edged
caps of this type.

★ KIRUNA AND GÄLLIVARE ★
ELECTRIC MIGHT IN THE LAND OF THE LAPPS

INTO this picturesque land has come a tremendous new force that is revolutionizing life in Swedish Lapland. It is cheap electricity.

Both literally and figuratively the communities, large and small, have been electrified. Now during the dark winter months, when the sun disappears for weeks or months at a time, depending on how far south you are, towns like Kiruna and Gällivare (two of the most important) are brilliantly lighted for twenty-four hours a day. Thousands of lights blaze forth, illuminating the snow-covered cottages which line the streets, the snow reflecting and intensifying the brightness which challenges the Arctic night.

Electricity is so cheap in Swedish Lapland that the people in their enthusiasm have strewn electric lights across the outskirts of towns where folks seldom venture, and even the mountains are illuminated. The twin mountains of Kirunavaara and Luossavaara are lit from base to peak, and Malmberget is ringed by lights for miles around, like some fairyland.

In the towns most kitchens and homes are completely electrified. In Kiruna, where the sun stays below the horizon for more than a month in midwinter, school children receive ultra-violet ray treatments as they study, to "make up for the lack of sunshine."

Not only does plentiful electricity change the Polar night into day and supply manufactured sunlight to children, it also makes possible the development of iron mines that are among the richest in the world. Electric plants give power to a completely electrified railroad, about 350 miles long, three-fourths of which is north of the Arctic Circle.

Water power is the secret of this magic that extracts the rich iron ore from the fabulous Kiruna and Gällivare mines, that gives motion to the freight and passenger trains of the state-owned railroad, that streaks in peace time through Arctic Sweden northwest and west through Arctic Norway to the ice-free port of Narvik.

About 800 rail miles north of Stockholm, and about 30 north of the Arctic Circle, the water from a string of lakes once climaxed at Porjus Falls in a series of rapids which sloped downward two miles. Here on the Lulea River, as early as 1914, dynamos were making the power that translates into work and speed, into heat and light. Since then the plant has been enlarged gradually. Today, with nearby plants, it supplies one-twelfth of all Sweden's hydro-electric energy.

The rapids have now been replaced by a dam almost a mile long and especially built to withstand the pressure of the lake ice, which freezes each winter to a depth of several yards, and to receive the tremendous late spring torrents. Below the surface of the lake a distributing basin has been excavated out of the solid rock, and an intake tunnel almost 2,000 feet long has been drilled to a roofed-over reservoir of seven chambers, each of which may be separately cut off by sluice gates. A drop of 164 feet down a shaft leads the water into seven turbine tubes, after passing through which it enters a drain tunnel and once again flows into the Lulea River. Most of this process takes place far below the reach of the most penetrating frost. A half-dozen or even a dozen feet of ice on the lake above will cause no freezing trouble below.

Except for the switch-house and nearby engineer's quarters, the Porjus plant is practically invisible. The power house, 160 feet below the surface of the earth, is pleasantly warmed by the natural heat of its dynamos throughout the winter. It, too, was blasted from the rock. The huge generator hall is built within a shell of reinforced concrete standing free from the surrounding rock so that moisture cannot penetrate its walls, and is as imposing as the underground crypt of some vast and ancient cathedral.

At the Porjus plant a network of colored cables less than an inch in

The midnight sun now illuminates symbols of modern electric power in Sweden's Arctic.

diameter lies at the opposite pole of the huge dam and the first intake tunnel. Through these slender cables travels the stream of power that does much of the work of the northern half of Sweden. And that is a good deal, in that highly electrified country.

A small town has grown up around the power plant at Porjus and most of the population depends on the station for a livelihood. Living standards are high.

An additional industry, a large electrified ore refinery, has been built at Gällivare. Inferior grades of ore are treated and then shipped south to local Swedish industry. In 1937 an inland railroad was completed, and Porjus is now a stop on the new line from Gällivare to Stockholm.

Porjus is not the only good power site in the Swedish Far North. A few miles below it is one that is potentially equally good, and nearby is another far larger. In other words, more power can be developed as it is needed, more than the northern half of Sweden could possibly use; but by connecting Porjus to the southern State power grid, which supplies one-third of the country's electrical energy, it can be used throughout the whole country. A trunk line is already being pushed northward to effect the union.

The southern rivers of Sweden have their heaviest flow of water in the winter season and are low in summer, while the opposite is true of the north; so the experts visualize a nice balance when the connection is made. Sweden, already one of the world's foremost manufacturing nations, will then be in a stronger position than ever before; and much of her strength will be coming from the Arctic.

The enormously rich mineral deposits of Swedish Lapland, which give it such strategic importance, are no recent discovery. As early as the fifteenth century, mines were in operation north of the Arctic Circle, but in most cases their success was short lived. Many times the kings of Sweden lent encouragement and assistance to adventurers willing to try their luck in the "wilderness," and several times there resulted short periods of prosperity, during which propaganda and inducement vied with each other to lure men North. Each time the seemingly insurmountable problems of transportation, labor, and living conditions brought failure.

In the sixteenth century the historian Johannes Shefferus argued that here in Sweden's Far North, rather than in the unknown territories of the Americas, lay the new lands Europe was so anxious to develop.

In the early part of the next century stories of fabulous riches to be had for the taking were circulated, and expanded with each telling. To solve the labor problem Lapps, still unchristianized and "untouched by civilization," were rounded up for forced labor. Swedes from the south, convicted of thievery, tax-evading and embezzlement, were offered work in the North in lieu of punishment. But the only means of shipping ore and of provisioning the workers was through the use of small reindeer-drawn sleighs which had to cross mountain range after mountain range, hundreds of miles of windswept tundra and long stretches of thickly forested wild land to reach their destinations.

Soon, alas, it was found that Lapland was not living up to its name of the Swedish Peru. Silver, copper and gold had not yet been found, and the rumored diamond fields existed only in the imaginations of wishful thinkers. In the Torne River valley a few settlements survived the bursting of the bubble, but it was the less romantic iron, which had been discovered in huge quantities, that sustained them. A local ore processing plant, established in 1646, started a small manufacturing industry. A little farther North, at what is today Gällivare, a parallel situation developed. For 150 years both settlements struggled along on a small scale, supplying the local blacksmiths and iron works.

Despite constant disappointment, the Swedes never quite lost faith in Lapland. Commissions to study and plan future developments of the country were at work periodically; a policy of encouraging settlement of the Far North was stubbornly continued, with little success.

In 1825 the first serious plans for constructing a railroad to the rich ore fields were presented. The cost would be enormous. So, after consideration, it was decided that the ore would never justify the construction of the road. For one thing, the ore contained a high percentage of phosphorous, which necessitated blending it with ores of different qualities before a good grade of iron could be obtained.

It was the discovery of the Thomas process that marked the dawn of a new era for Lapland. It is a treatment through which the high phosphorous content of Lappish ore ceased to be a drawback; on the contrary, it turned out to be a distinct advantage, resulting in a superior product. Furthermore the treatment produced a by-product, Thomas Phosphate, which itself had money value.

In the early eighteen eighties a British-Swedish syndicate had obtained the concession to construct a railroad from Lulea, on the Baltic, to the rich Gällivare mining districts, and by 1890 the first part of it was nearing completion. The public in Sweden wanted the state to take over and continue the road straight across Lapland to the Norwegian border; for it had been discovered that the mountains of Kirunavaara and Luossavaara* contained concentrated wealth far beyond previous wildest expectations. The Swedish Parliament approved the plans for extending the railway, bought the existing line from Lulea to Gällivare, and entered into an agreement with Norway regarding the extension of the road across the narrow Norwegian strip to the Atlantic.

The completion of the railroad from Gällivare to Narvik, on Norway's coast, in 1902, was considered one of the outstanding engineering feats of its day. Rail now extended northwestward from the Baltic Sea across the whole of the Scandinavian Peninsula, with Gällivare at about the center and Kiruna somewhat farther northward. It meant, too, a year-round ice-free port, Narvik, as an ocean shipping point. This was a great advantage. Lulea could be used only during summer, as the North Baltic is frozen during middle and late winter. Ore could now be shipped in either or both directions as needed.

The Thomas process had, in effect, bestowed quality upon Lappish ore. The railroad solved transportation. There remained only the problem of labor.

While politicians were arguing the pros and cons of investing the taxpayers' money in developing Lapland's resources, Dr. Hjalmar Lundbohm, "Lapland's Uncrowned King," went quietly to work. It was he, a geologist, who was the first to foresee the tremendous possibilities for transforming Kirunavaara and Luossavaara into modern settlements. At the site of present day Kiruna he built himself a log house, at the foot of the mountain, and there worked out the plans for an ideal future community. It was his belief that if the right type of worker was to be attracted, practical and comfortable homes must be waiting to welcome him. The finest Swedish engineers, architects and designers were invited to visit the town site and, with Lundbohm, they planned it to the last detail.

When the first workers arrived at Kiruna in 1903 and 1904, they found an attractive modern city awaiting them, with bright new houses and schools

---

* Kirunavaara is Lappish for Grouse Mountain; Luosavaara means Salmon Mountain.

(*above*) Dynamite for mine blasting is stored in these cellars. (*below*) Night scene.

(above) A modern Kiruna house stands behind this barrier of logs, built to ease the shock of daily dynamite explosions. Only houses near the mine are so protected. (below) Electrically operated scoops are used for mining at Kirunavaara.

Winter scene at Kiruna.

considered by some to be the finest in Sweden. The school children received from the very start free medical and dental care, as well as free hot lunches. When a miner finished his day's work, he found a locker in which to leave his dirty clothes, a Finnish bath to remove the accumulated grime, and a free street car waiting to take him home—and to bring him back again next day. There was a fully-equipped hospital, a club with recreational facilities and, the pride of the town, an imposing church of Lapp-style architecture, picturesquely placed at the edge of a large wooded park.

Wage standards were among the highest in the world, with paid vacations and adequate social security measures. This was in 1904, long before the words "social security" had become part of the American vocabulary. In the past, Lapland had suffered from shiftless workers, ne'er-do-wells, get-rick-quick adventurers. Kiruna was the answer; time proved it to be a good one. Few of those who found work here ever returned south.

In 1909 Kiruna was incorporated and granted a city charter. It then had a population of ten thousand and was the biggest inland town in the world north of the circle. Today it has about 15,000.

Kiruna in summer is not very different from more southerly Swedish towns.

While Kiruna was being planned in deliberate and orderly fashion, Gällivare, the rich ore district to the south, was passing through a hectic period comparable to the early days of our Wild West. The various ore fields were owned by different groups, some of whom were interested in the project only as a speculation.

Here no provision was made for the thousands of workers who, attracted by the high wages, descended on the settlement. Gällivare and Malmberget, just north of it, mushroomed overnight in best Gold Rush tradition. With only a handful of buildings to start with, makeshift shelters were constructed from old packing cases and barrels, and people lived in crude dugouts. The feverish construction of dwellings that followed was completely haphazard and ignored all suggestion of town planning. But the town prospered, nevertheless, for the resources were great and the nearby success of Kiruna was a permanent bulwark, an ever-shining lodestar. The advantages of careful town planning were tardily realized and attempts made to erase the blunders of those first mad days, but it was many years before the last scars were effaced.

The completely electrified railway is state owned and operates throughout the year.

In some prehistoric age, the iron ore of Kiruna, which is of the black magnetic kind, of unusually fine quality, was melted and raised to the surface by some gigantic force, to form twin mountains of solid iron nearly half a mile high, Kirunavaara and Luossavaara. Kiruna Mountain alone, it has been said by competent judges, is able to supply the normal demand of the whole world for 250 years. A conservative estimate of its known ore has been put at one thousand million tons. It is not known how far down the iron goes, but diamond drillings have reached 2700 feet and still found solid iron ore. Combined with Luossavaara and Gällivare, Kirunavaara forms one of the largest and richest iron ore deposits in the whole world. Kiruna's vein of iron is about two miles long and runs to the very peak of the mountain, so that instead of having to delve underground for the ore, actual mining is carried out on terraces cut right into the mountain side.

Day after day, car after car, and train after train of iron ore emerges in a steady stream from Kirunavaara, pausing only on Sundays, and on the very few days in winter when the fresh snowfall is too heavy for the trains to operate.

71

Three times each day, except Sunday, at 8:40 A.M., 12:20 P.M., and 4:00 P.M., red lights flash in and near the mines, red flags are run up for miles around the blasting area, and sirens scream, echoing and re-echoing through the hills in a crescendo of sound. This is the signal announcing that the dynamite, packed in holes made by compressed-air drills, is about to be blasted. The explosions shake the countryside, rattling the windows in the town of Kiruna three miles away. Dust and smoke hide the upper part of the mountain after the blast, as the townfolk remove the wadding from their ears and settle back to the day's routine.

Not merely are the blasts on the minute, the whole mining operation is a masterpiece of timing and ingenious design. Workers get busy on the terraces after each blast with heavy electric cranes, each of which can pick up pieces of ore weighing ten tons. Twenty of these, each operated by a single man, are directed over a maze of tracks to the newly blasted ore. While the cranes are busy, ore cars are being assembled into small trains, with clocklike precision.

Five cars, each with a twenty-five-ton capacity, are pulled by one small electric locomotive. When the cars are filled, the train moves across the terrace to the crush shafts, which stand in a row of five, one for each car. Here the ore is dumped and falls with terrific force on cross pieces in the shaft which break it into lumps of six feet or less. These in turn continue falling and are broken again into the required smaller size. The crushed ore at last falls into the big loading shafts that extend perpendicularly down through the mountain. The bottom of the loading shaft connects with a railroad tunnel about two miles long which leads to the outside world. Here empty ore cars come in on one track, filled cars leave by another.

The empty cars are automatically weighed as they pull up to the loading shaft and their weight registered. At the rate of one second per ton they are filled. When each contains thirty-five tons, a light and sound signal stops the loading and the next car moves up. A sample of ore is taken from each car as it leaves the tunnel for the Kiruna Ore Railway Yards, which are outside Kiruna proper, to the west.

Thirty loaded trains, each composed of twenty thirty-five-ton cars, a total of 600 cars, emerge from the tunnel each day. They are turned over to the State Railway to be made up into long-haul ore trains. In peace time at least twenty trains of forty cars each, drawn by powerful electric locomotives, are dispatched each twenty-four-hour day throughout the year, to

Narvik or to Lulea.

Through a countryside where pack reindeer, and reindeer sleighs, were formerly the only means of transportation, there now races the most northerly electrified railroad in the world. With up-to-date equipment second to none, and powered by Porjus's underground hydro-electric plant, it brings some of the world's richest iron ore to shipping terminals whence it is dispatched to far corners of the globe.

From Kiruna to Narvik, from Kiruna to Lulea—the railroad dashes across Scandinavia in all weathers.

THE early history of Siberia is a story of fur, and no wonder, when two black fox pelts in the early seventeenth century would bring one hundred and ten rubles. With that sum you could buy fifty-five acres of land, build a good cabin, acquire five horses, twenty head of cattle, twenty sheep, several dozen fowl and still have half your capital left. Sable and ermine skins, too, lured combination exploring and trading expeditions farther and farther eastward from Moscow, until they reached the Pacific Ocean, *four thousand miles away.*

The swiftness of progress eastward was determined by the abundance of furs in the last outpost. As the supply diminished, the next easy step was movement into the rich, untouched areas beyond. Portages connected the mighty northward-flowing Siberian rivers all the way to Bering Sea, and with the smaller branches provided transport in almost any needed direction.

The chief trader in this vast enterprise was the Moscow Government itself. A tribute or tax in furs was collected from the native Tungus, Samoyeds, and Ostiaks, and a ten per cent tax, payable in the finest furs was collected from all private traders and trappers, so the state collected "coming and going." The Government also retained for itself the right to buy the finest furs of merchant and trapper alike, and, with a monopoly on the

74

sables and black fox sold to China, developed a lucrative foreign trade. Russian furs found their way to Leipzig and Chinese fur markets and were the most important single item in all sixteenth century Russian commerce, both foreign and domestic.

Siberia poured most of this wealth into the Government's coffers. Remember that every tenth skin caught by a native went to the Czar, and it is easy to see why he was as interested as any merchant for the fur industry to expand. The incredible riches to be gained almost overnight explain why men were willing to endure untold hardships, and even risk death to push on to unexplored richer areas, where new tribes would trap the precious, furry animals for them.

From that romantic period until the end of the nineteenth century, intrepid explorers of many nations tried again and again to make the Northeast Passage around Siberia, to link the Atlantic and Pacific Oceans from the North, instead of following the longer existing route around the Cape of Good Hope. The navigation of the Northeast Passage in 1878 was hailed as an heroic feat. Today the passage is being utilized as a regular commercial highway every year, by many ships, despite the short season of three months during which the waters north of Siberia are open and navigable.

Soon after the Revolution strange things began to happen in this country that once saw only an occasional explorer or trapper. Towns and villages suddenly mushroomed along the coast and at the mouths of the great rivers. From the Kola Peninsula to Bering Strait, they were linked together by radio stations, and intersected by airplane routes. New industries were developed, new ports built to accommodate the resultant shipping. A system of ice-reporting was invented which combined with ice-breakers to see that ships got in and out of their ports at their appointed times. Under the direction of the Northern Sea Route Administration, virtual ruler of the Soviet North, the four existing meteorological stations were expanded to more than sixty, and sprinkled along the routes of navigation and throughout the furthest outposts of the Soviet Arctic.

To a ship's captain in this region the ice report means what a weather report means to a flyer. The Soviet technique of ice reconnaissance, or ice reporting, has transformed their formerly useless Arctic Sea into a busy seaway. Aided by the numerous polar stations and a fleet of scouting planes, a system has been invented which, in many ways, resembles our weather

75

forecasting, except that it is the movement of the ice, rather than that of clouds and low pressure areas, which is reported upon. Long and short flights are made and observations taken to determine the thickness of the pack ice, the direction in which it is going, and how fast it is moving.

Here is the way it works. A ship's captain radios the nearest polar station and asks for an ice report, and as it is radioed back, he plots it on a base map. He does this several times a day, and soon has a pretty accurate picture of the position and movement of the ice pack in his vicinity, and how to avoid it. Now it often happens that when one side of a strait is impassable with heavy ice, the other is free and open. It is no longer a matter of guess work for the skipper to decide which side to try. Instead of depending on the limited vision of a seaman in the crow's nest (the old fashioned way of having a look at the ice) a captain has the benefit of the horizon of a moving airplane a thousand or more feet in the air. When all stations and scouting planes have reported in to a central station, an amazingly accurate forecast is the result. According to Leningrad's Arctic Institute, the 1939 forecasts of the East Siberian Sea were eighty-three per cent accurate, and they consider ice reporting to be in its infancy!

Ice-breakers are the trouble-shooters of the Northeast Passage. Their main function is of course to open, and keep open, certain straits in the paths of the merchant ships, and this is possible when the ice is young and not too thick. They are powerless against the terrific force of heavy pack ice—there ice reporting comes to the rescue. Instead of fighting the mighty pack, which can crush a ship as if it were made of paper, a ship now avoids it. It may have to sail hundreds of miles off its course to stay clear of the ice, but it arrives eventually without having run the constant danger of being trapped and destroyed.

Some ice-breakers have been temporarily fitted up as floating observatories, carrying men and women scientists and their assistants to unknown areas of the northern sea, where they study its temperature and saltiness, the direction and force of its currents, and the habits of the numerous living things that make their homes in it. Ice-breakers have even discovered new land, but for the most part they are dashing off to the aid of a ship accidently caught in the ice. When they have freed it, off they go to clear a path for a convoy of merchant ships homeward bound, perhaps from Igarka with a cargo of lumber, perhaps from the Lena River with a cargo of gold, or from Nordvyk with a load of salt.

(above) The ice-breaker "Yermak" among heavy floes. *(below)* The captain of the "Sedov" discusses a message with the wireless operator.

(*above*) The "Stalin," king of the Soviet ice-breaker fleet, approaches the ice-imprisoned "Sedov" at night in order to free her. (*below*) In the Greenland Sea the crew of the "Stalin" clears the ice from her decks and ropes.

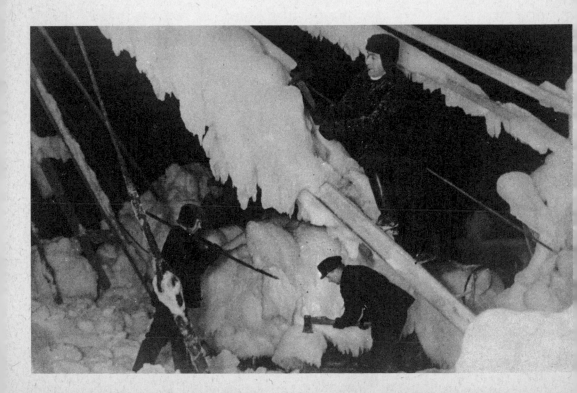

(*above*) The "Sedov" ahoy! (*below*) Drawing alongside the rescued ship. This is in mid-winter about 900 miles north of the Arctic Circle.

(*above*) The Northern Sea Route Administration trains women as well as men for the Arctic Merchant Marine. This is a class in hydro-meteorology. (*below*) These young girls, natives of the Soviet Arctic, study at Leningrad in a specially created Institute for five years. Then they return to their northern homes perhaps as teachers, agronomists, zoologists or government officials.

Determined to make the frozen earth yield up its coal, oil, gold, silver, platinum, nickel and other minerals, the virgin forests their timber, and the sea its fish, an era of industralization was inaugurated throughout the Soviet Arctic by its government. The U.S.S.R. has the largest stake of all the countries within the Circle, for it occupies forty-nine per cent of the land surrounding the Polar Mediterranean. Professor Otto Schmidt, Arctic hero and vice president of the Academy of Sciences, has summed up his country's attitude toward their High North. He says "not only does our country believe in Vilhjalmur Stefansson's 'Friendly Arctic', we are making friends with it, bringing it to life, and life to it."

One of the numerous polar stations splashed across the Red North is the most northerly in all the world. It is at Rudolf Island in Franz Josef Land (latitude 82° N). Here, as at all other stations, scientific workers probe and poke into every branch of Arctic science, methodically gathering information to be published later by the Arctic Institute of Leningrad. A polar station may have a staff of anywhere from a handful to hundreds, depending on its location and importance. Weather and ice observations are taken regularly, queries from ships and planes answered and radio beam signals sent out. Because of the labor shortage many of the scientists have been trained with alternate skills, and it is not unusual for a staff physician to be also a trained weather observer, a radio operator, a graduate meteorologist, and so on.

A wife cannot accompany her husband to his post at a polar station unless she, too, is a trained scientist. Single women workers often find romance at these outposts, marry some fellow investigator and raise families. Children born and raised at these faraway places frolic in sun and snow, finding simple pleasures in much the same fashion as southern children. With the same tense excitement provoked in a city child by the balloon man at the circus, they watch breathlessly the release of stratosphere balloons which rise high up into the atmosphere, sending down radio reports for an hour or two before they disappear forever into space.

Perhaps you think a polar station, isolated as it is, would be a pretty dull place to live and work. Recreational facilities of all sorts provided for spare hours, however, make the time pass all too quickly. All the stations have libraries, some with as many as five thousand volumes. More than twenty-three stations print their own newspapers (as do ice-breakers, and other Arctic ships) and "wall newspapers" are encountered everywhere, even at the smallest fur trading post. There are dark rooms for amateur photographers; musical instruments, phonographs and radios for music lovers and newshounds. Those who enjoy the outdoor life hunt fox, polar bear, seal and any other animals in the vicinity, combining pleasurable exercise with securing a fresh food supply. The country's outstanding Arctic heroes have written accounts of their northern work which are widely distributed in pamphlet form and stimulate a great deal of interest in the North. The result has been far more applications for northern posts than openings to be filled.

To help the natives of the Far North over the hump of adjusting from the stone to the air age, with practically no intermediate period, the Institute for the Peoples of the North was founded in Leningrad in 1926. Its first students, coming from every part of the Soviet Arctic, arrived, some in deer-skin clothes, and shyly met their neighbors, many of them for the first time. Yakuts met Evenki, Chukchi met nomads from the Taimyr and Kola Peninsulas, and discovered common interests but found their languages were different. With the aid of trained linguists, the early students helped prepare alphabets for sixteen primitive languages which formerly had none, and when they returned home as qualified teachers, they taught their pupils to read and write in their own tongue as well as in Russian.

Regardless of which of the thirty ethnic groups they belonged to, all natives of the Soviet North had the privilege of entering any profession on an equal basis with the half million others in the Far North. Many have been trained as doctors, nurses, teachers, meteorologists and even as airplane pilots. Their brightest youngsters are sent to Leningrad for training and upon gradu-tion most of them return to practice and teach what they have learned.

And so we see that Siberia, traditional home of howling wolves and exiles, frozen wastes and impossible cold, has had a change of face. The territories are still vast, but now they are linked by radio, ships and airplanes. The climate is still cold, for the thermometer goes 90° below zero at Verk-hoyansk, but it gets still colder at Oimekon two hundred miles south of the Circle, where people survive and live a normal span of life. In the Soviet Arctic the myth of the useless frozen North has been shattered forever. Now pioneers are adapting themselves to the country and overcoming its obstacles, learning to harness and make use of its many good things.

Releasing a pilot-balloon from an ice airdrome at the North Pole during the Papanin Expedition. *(below)* An aerologist at a polar station records the readings of a meteorograph before sending it skyward with a kite.

(*above*) The Nensti are only one of many peoples that inhabit the Soviet North. (*below*) Sparse vegetation of a sandflat on one of the islands in the mouth of the Lena River.

A group of students at the Institute for Northern Peoples. Notice the mural in the background showing the use of sledge reindeer.

★ IGARKA ★

SIBERIA'S BOOM TOWN

IGARKA, the "magic" city of Arctic Siberia, is the youngest and most startling Polar metropolis in the world, the unofficial capital of the Siberian Arctic. Once a paragraph in a first Five Year Plan, it is today the living symbol of an era of Arctic pioneering unprecedented in history, more vast in scale than the opening of our West.

As you steam up the wide Yenisei River to Igarka, its little wooden houses of bright, natural yellow pine gleam in the sunlight, and the sweet, fragrant smell of newly-sawn wood, that envelops the town, is borne riverward by the wind to greet you. This piquant aroma comes from the town's three sawmills, where husky, red-cheeked girls, their hair tied up in white handkerchiefs, guide the lumber toward the beautiful and frighteningly sharp Swedish steel saws that screech and groan during the operation. This pleasant wood smell is the town's trademark and whenever and wherever you encounter it again, a pang of recognition will recreate Igarka for you as vividly as any photograph.

Another unforgettable smell which cannot be disassociated from any Siberian town is the delicious scent of newly baked bread, which the Russians make with molasses. Long before you reach the bakery the mouth-watering odor reaches you, and if it is a cold morning and you haven't breakfasted, your nostrils will probably start to quiver, and you will feel like breaking into a run, to taste a warm thick slice of it the sooner.

Our account of Igarka is gleaned from information that came to us before 1938. By that year the Soviets were already beginning to prepare for the war they feared was inevitable and all news of Igarka ceased. When war came, more than ever before women undoubtedly took over the jobs of men as they were called to the front. It is possible that with the evacuation of factories and families to Siberia both new people and machines found their way to Igarka. It is even conceivable that with an expanded population, activity in the town surpassed pre-war days. But this is speculation. Here instead is how it was before we had to guess, at the time when Igarka was young and growing with the incredible speed of a baby in its first year.

From a tiny settlement of one house and three natives, Igarka grew to a busy, teeming industrial center of twenty thousand in a short period of less than ten years. Despite the fact that it lies sixty-seven miles north of the Circle, it is today one of the most important Arctic seaports, a gateway through which Siberia's tremendous wealth can reach the markets of the world.

For hundreds of years Russia understood dimly the urgent need for an ice-free outlet for her northward flowing Siberian Rivers, to release from isolation their vast and fertile valleys. Little was accomplished along practical lines. Then the Soviet Government began to plan and develop its Far Northern regions on the premise that industries in the Arctic were both possible and profitable. Igarka seems to vindicate their claim.

Perhaps one reason for the drastic change in policy between the regime of the Czars and the new government, was that Josef Stalin had spent part of a period of exile on the Yenisei, hard by the Arctic Circle, so that he understood the nature of the country and climate, and grasped the importance of developing a more adequate seaway connection between the Atlantic and Pacific Oceans.

When the Soviets came to power ships were not having any difficulty reaching the Yenisei, but they went in with heavy loads and came back empty. A most uneconomical procedure. Something had to be found to provide a return cargo. Explorers were dispatched to prospect for such cargoes and they decided in favor of lumber. Igarka was chosen to become a lumbering center, blue prints were drawn up for the town, machinery was ordered—things began to hum on the Yenisei.

One of the good reasons for selecting Igarka was that here the main waters of the Yenisei are divided by long Bear's Island, which offers shelter for a perfect natural harbor· Although four hundred miles south of the Polar Sea, ocean-going vessels may steam up the broad river and anchor here in deep and sheltered waters.

As Igarka symbolizes and dominates the Siberian Arctic, so does timber symbolize and dominate Igarka.

Siberia's forests of merchantable timber are considered the finest in the world and are as large as half the United States. Here are pines so straight and tall that a ship's mast can be fashioned from a single trunk. Trees by the thousand million to be turned miraculously into newsprint, plywood, cellulose, rayon, nylon. While the reserves of the finer sort of timber are being steadily depleted in most countries, it has been said that the forests of Siberia are so vast that even if they were ruthlessly cut down, as many of ours were in earlier days still her abundance could supply the world for two or three centuries.

The wood shipped from Igarka is of so fine a quality that, just before the war, London merchants had to purchase a prescribed quantity of other Soviet woods in order to get some of the preferred Yenisei lumber.

But riches of this kind are profitable in commerce only if there is a handy waterway to transport the logs. Shipping by rail would cost too much.

Like most of Siberia's great rivers, the Yenisei flows northward, so the procedure adopted to get timber to where it is needed is first to float the logs down river to Igarka's sawmills and then to carry the lumber on northward by steamers to the Arctic Sea. Here some of the steamers turn east, to go part way or the whole way to the Pacific; most of them head west, for the Atlantic, and through its waters to Europe, Africa, South and North America.

The ships that carry away Yenisei lumber between June and September have been plying other waters the winter before. These steamers, foreign and Soviet, head for Igarka from western seas in the early summer, bringing machinery, food and other necessities. They sail from their widely separated harbors, in Europe and elsewhere, to the Kara Sea of the Soviet Arctic. Here they are met by an ice-breaker which, like a duck at the head of her brood,

Timber, floated downstream along the northward flowing Yenisei, arrives at Igarka.

leads the convoy through the scattered ice of the Kara Sea and then up the Yenisei. After they unload they are re-provisioned, and with the aid of Igarka's fleet of American built lumber trucks, their holds are filled with seasoned timber which they carry off to far corners of the earth.

With the supply of wood so abundant, it is not surprising that almost everything in Igarka is made of it. Not only the yellow log cabins, but all the public buildings are made of wood. The theatre, the clubs, the movie house, the fire station and the Port Authority building are all built according to the modern so-called "Functional" school of architecture, but the use of timber, rather than concrete or brick, gives them a warm, comfortable look.

The first buildings erected in the "old" part of town mysteriously sagged or collapsed and are rapidly being abandoned. Hastily built, their floors were close to the ground, and no allowance was made for the frozen subsoil. At Igarka, as in a large part of Siberia, the ground three to eight feet below the surface is permanently frozen; it never thaws, even in summer. The heat from the stoves warming the new houses soon began to thaw the frozen ground and the foundations gradually sank into the soft mud.

A freighter takes on a cargo of logs.

The trouble was soon diagnosed and a simple treatment prescribed. An air space is now provided between the floor of the house and the ground so that cold air can circulate freely and *prevent* the ground from thawing. Frozen mud is as hard as concrete; so long as it remains frozen it is an excellent foundation for a house, for the paving of a road, or the surface of an airport. The special problems connected with frozen subsoil, or "permafrost," are studied at a research station at Igarka devoted solely to study, research and testing in this new scientific field.

Even the sidewalks of our Polar metropolis are made of wood, and look much like those in our early western towns, indeed like those still found in northerly Alaskan or Canadian hamlets.

Before the war, walking resoundingly along Igarka's well-polished boards, which protect you from the icy ground in winter and the swamp-like mud in summer, you met attractive, well-dressed, busy young people. Some were newly arrived from a far corner of the Soviet Union, attracted by the high wages, which were in Igarka's first years much higher than at Moscow or in any ordinary Soviet town. Others, idealists, and there were a great many of these, had come inspired by the thought of making the Arctic fruitful and pushing still farther northward the outermost boundary of a livable, workable world. Still others, who liked to conquer obstacles, came because there was a tremendous job of work to be done and they knew their skills would find full scope.

As we have said, Igarka was built from scratch. When the first crew of two thousand workers arrived in 1929, only a few stayed behind during the winter, living in temporary shelters until the permanent ones were constructed. The next summer the procedure was repeated, but thereafter more and more summer workers began to spend the winter, too, until the permanent population numbered twenty thousand.

During Igarka's early years, about forty per cent of her residents were *kulaks,* or forced immigrants who had refused to join the collective farms voluntarily.

Formerly these kulaks had been prosperous landlords, many of them with tenants of their own. After the Revolution, as the socialization of the country went forward apace, the collectives were constantly granted more advantages, the kulaks had fewer and fewer. Life became difficult for these unhappy and, by now, embittered men. Finally, by decree or by decision of the village Soviets, the kulaks were deprived of their property, which was turned over to the community, and many were exiled. Some were taken to Igarka to help build it, as forced workers. Most of these were five-year exiles.

During the construction of Igarka there was little to distinguish from the free men the kulaks who were doing forced labor. Their food, clothing, housing, wages and manners were the same, and they had the freedom of the town. About the only restrictions imposed were that they could not leave town, they could not take part in political meetings. Any conspicuously good work on their part resulted in shortening of sentences, or complete pardon; many in Igarka had regained their full citizenship on that basis before it was granted to all kulaks by the new constitution.

In 1936 there were four thousand former kulaks in Igarka. The civil rights of all had been restored, as rewards or by constitutional reform, and they were now accepted into the community.

When Igarka was six years old, who carried the main responsibility for the proper functioning of this city which had challenged the Arctic and won? For its sawmills, its graphite factory whose workers looked like chimney sweeps, its chemical plant, its fishing industry and its precious furs? Some young Siberian giant, some hoary scientist from the Arctic Institute of Leningrad, bursting with theories to be tested? No! Surprisingly to us, though not to the people of the Soviet Union, the virtual dictator of Igarka was a woman.

From her bright, three-story wooden City Hall, Velentina Petrovna Ostroumova, a woman in her early forties with the figure of a girl, supervised the destinies of Igarka's twenty thousand. In the blue naval uniform of the Northern Sea Route Administration, she was to be seen down at the docks giving commands to the captain of a vessel; discussing an editorial for Igarka's newspaper with the author; or drinking tea with a group of visiting officials.

With her arrival in February, 1935, the city seemed to have a sudden access of new power that resulted in booming production. With incredible energy, she worked until three o'clock in the morning, and yet was often up at five and at her desk. Although heartily disliked by some of the captains and engineers of the old school, who still believed in the old slogan that "a woman's place is in the home" and who resented taking orders from a woman, the majority of the workers liked Ostroumova. Many of the women imitated her; everybody respected her sincerity and industry.

That Igarka had a woman for "mayor" was nothing exceptional. From the start, Soviet women have taken an active part in politics, science, agriculture, in nearly every line of endeavor. Equal pay for equal work, the old feminist slogan, has real meaning here; for not only is the pay equal but so is the work. Igarka's women have built houses, sawed wood, loaded and unloaded ships, paved streets, working side by side with men. Many of the meteorologists in the North are women, and so are the doctors. Women are seamen, even captains of ships. The ice-breaker *Krassin* had a woman stoker and two women chemists aboard during one of her expeditions. Ruth Gruber, the first foreign correspondent to see Igarka, writes in *I Went to the Soviet Arctic*: "Women in Russia have long been working as long and as hard as men. Their short muscular bodies are not the sudden fruit of the Revolution."

One might think that all the women in Igarka are rugged Amazons, but that is not so. Some of them, usually the wives of the more highly paid engineers or sea captains, do no work at all but spend much of their time at social activities and in making themselves and their homes more attractive.

Only two years after the first settlers of Igarka arrived, a small group of scientists and their helpers came there from Moscow and Leningrad. No sooner had they pitched their tents, across the harbor on Bear's Island, than

Igarka's agricultural experiment station.

work began feverishly. They were professors and students from agricultural institutes who had come north determined to make green things grow on Igarka's tundra. With the help of husky townsmen, the newcomers cleared the ground of its abundant Arctic vegetation of bushes, grasses, mosses, lichens, and proceeded to plant potatoes, lettuce, grain, radishes and beetroots in tiny experimental plots of ground.

Few of the residents believed that these scientists would ever grow anything edible, and the first two years seemed to confirm this belief. But in 1932, after a change of method, the first small crop of Arctic potatoes and radishes was harvested, giving new courage to the experimenters and breaking down the resistance of the "doubting Thomases."

93

By now *Transarctica,* as the farm is called, is an assured success, and taken for granted by the townsfolk. Its potatoes, onions, carrots and cabbages, grown in the open fields, are sold in the stores and arouse no comment from the shoppers. And not only does the farm supply the town; there is a surplus and part of it is flown northward to the Polar stations on the Arctic coast of the mainland and in the islands of the northern sea. Each year about five hundred new experiments are tried. An average of thirty or forty prove successful, which is deemed satisfactory by the agriculturists.

The chief agriculturist, Marie Mitrofanovna Khrenikova, is a middle-aged woman. With four young girl students, who live in a cottage surrounded by pansies, forget-me-nots and pinks, she does observation work. Every hour the temperatures of the soil, the subsoil and the air is recorded. Carefully they measure and register the average daily moisture and the total daily amount of sunlight.

As Marie Mitrofanovna shows you her cauliflower and lettuce, grown in hotbeds under showcases of glass, she has all the enthusiasm and pleasure of a collector of rare books showing you his Shakespeare first folio.

Aside from the crops of the open field some others, among them cucumbers, tomatoes, asparagus and flowers, are grown in crowded hothouses. The growing season is from seventy to one hundred days at Igarka, much as at Alaska's Fort Yukon; the long stretches of sunshine, from twenty-four hours down to twenty per day in the frostless period, make the crops grow quickly and to large sizes, compensating for the brevity of the summer when measured in weeks. According to optimistic Marie Mitrofanovna, they will be growing cereals, and she is looking forward to growing watermelons, too, some day.

The hothouses at *Transarctica* have fur-lined doors! Built of brick, lined with wooden beams to keep the temperature constant, they are half buried underground. Large clay stoves, burning Igarka's plentiful wood, have radiators running along all the walls. Heat is hoarded by carefully filling all cracks with cotton wool, seaweed or cloth. It is in this cause that the doors are fur-lined. Steep glass windows gather all the natural light available for the plants growing on shelves beneath them.

The main aim of the Polar farm, with its four hundred head of cattle and its three hundred and sixty large white English pigs, is not to try to make an agricultural country of the Yenisei valley but to grow enough fresh vegetables for the town and to make the people self-sufficient should

The amount of precipitation is recorded by a farm meteorologist.

they ever be cut off from the rest of the country by sea and air.

One of the disconcerting things about Igarka, to a visitor, is that they run the city on Moscow time. With a difference of four hours between the clocks and the sun, a fatigued traveler arriving late at night, his head filled with pleasant thoughts of bed and sleep, will find to his astonishment that he is just in time for dinner and will probably not be allowed to retire for hours, especially if some celebration has been planned in his honor.

But with the continuous daylight of mid-summer the strange timing makes little difference to Igarkans, who seem to prefer it. They listen eagerly to the Moscow news broadcasts every day and would hate to have to wait until two in the morning to hear the Opera broadcast from the Bolshoi, equivalent of our Metropolitan Opera House. Newcomers soon get the hang of it, and learn to drink afternoon tea in the middle of the night without noticing the time.

"The Arctic Bolshevik" is the name of the town's daily newspaper. By eight o'clock each morning there are newsboys on the street distributing it. In 1936 it was a four-page illustrated affair which, during the navigation season, carried a supplement in English for the benefit of visiting merchant seamen. Although designed chiefly to inform visitors about Igarka and the Soviet North, the supplement would at times include English sport news, translated articles and items from the short wave radio which the editor thought would interest the foreign seamen.

The editorial offices were housed in a little cottage, with an annex containing the presses and cases of type; the skilled typesetter was a woman. Tass News Agency supplied spot news by telegraph and news was also picked up from the radio every day. The edition usually numbered around 3000. The paper contained frequent help-wanted ads but never any situations-wanted, reflecting the labor shortage. The weekly announcement of the new film to be seen at the movie house was the only paid advertisement. The dramatic column heralded long in advance the coming of the Polar Theatre to Igarka, and reported the actors' doings while they were in town.

When the Polar Theatre came to Igarka each summer before the war, a gala holiday feeling enveloped the town. It meant real actors, some of Moscow's finest, performing in the flesh and literally everyone in the city turned out for the event, children and babies included. Mothers left their young children in a special room presided over by a nurse, which enabled mother and audience to enjoy the performances undisturbed by childish howls which would be sure to occur in the most serious dramatic moments. The wooden theatre, with walls of soft shaded woods which were unpainted but waxed to a soft, warm gleam, throbbed with repressed excitement.

The actors of the Polar Theatre sacrificed their six-weeks holiday, which they were entitled to spend at some fashionable health resort, to come north, bringing to Igarka, and to places even more remote, their fine dramatic performances. If it is Molière's *Tartuffe* they are playing, it is performed exactly as it would be in Moscow, complete with satin knee breeches, powdered wigs and all. For compensation the actors have probably the most appreciative audiences in the world, since before the Polar Theatre came north, Igarkans had never seen a big-city type of production. All hang on every spoken word, weeping with the heroine for sadness or joy, guffawing at the jokes and booing the villain.

The actors don the uniform of Polar Workers before leaving Moscow, and as they promenade along the wooden sidewalks, they return the hundreds of greetings offered them by touching in salute the badge on their caps, the blue Arctic banner. The holiday air is infectious. During their stay the club auditorium at night is alive with holiday spirit and mixed languages as the sailors, townfolk and actors make merry.

As late as 1936, river water was still brought to each house by an ancient carrier who filled his huge, brown barrel each day and delivered the water, milkman style. But the next year Igarka was building water mains in the frozen ground. Cast iron water pipes were placed in shallow trenches lined with boards and surrounded with moss or sawdust. A steam pipe was placed alongside, to prevent the freezing of the mains. A sewage system was also planned and except for possible delay because of the war, this has doubtless been installed.

The night life of the town usually takes the form of visiting one of the three clubs, the largest of which has an auditorium seating about 1,000, equipped with a revolving stage. Two smaller ones can accommodate about two hundred each; both of these have athletic facilities and rifle galleries. All three have libraries, with books in all languages. During the navigation season one of the clubs is under the joint management of a Russian and of a Hamburg-born Australian sailor who has been appointed a kind of social director. He goes from ship to ship inviting sailors to visit the Polar farm, to go through the sawmills, to take part in a football game, or to attend a dance that evening at the club.

In a large room at the club, dinners are attended by Soviet and foreign seamen, speeches are made, ideas are exchanged. There is dancing afterwards. A smaller room, with soft shaded lights and comfortable sofas, offers a quiet place for seamen to play chess and dominoes while they sip wine. Igarka has no saloons. Liquor is sold only in bottles at regular stores and at such exorbitant prices that it is little used.

The cold winters don't seem to bother the inhabitants of our timber town much. Children attend school throughout the winter and play outdoors with little or no discomfort. The sawmills are shut down only when the thermometer drops lower than sixty degrees below zero. This seldom happens and better insulation of factory buildings will soon doubtless prevent even those rare shutdowns.

There are lots of children in Igarka. The state makes it as easy as possible for women to have healthy babies. It provides clean, free maternity hospitals as well as extra money for layettes and other maternity needs. Prenatal and postnatal care are also free.

From the time children are two months old until they are three years old they may be left in a crêche or day nursery until four o'clock in the afternoon. Between the ages of three and seven a youngster spends his days in kindergarten. Both arrangements are voluntary and mothers who do not work often keep their children at home with them.

Public school is free, and compulsory until the age of sixteen. Thereafter, if more learning is sought, there is the equivalent of our college at some city, like Krasnoyarsk or Novosibirsk, or Moscow. If at the end of collegiate training, perhaps about equivalent to graduation from one of our junior colleges, a student wants to specialize in some subject, he may go on to an institute for another four years.

To newcomers Igarka offered what had been, a few years before, unheard of opportunities. Many middle-aged couples learned to read and write during their first winter in this, the most cosmopolitan town they had ever seen. Some had their first glimpse of a big ocean-going steamer; some saw their first foreigners—East Indians, Hollanders, Scandinavians, Negroes, Englishmen—all of whom may be seen on the streets of Igarka when the ships are in. Laborers found a chance for education and better jobs; ambitious ones were always trying to acquire some new skill at night when their day's work was done. Youngsters could earn enough to marry on. Those with exceptional talents were noticed and perhaps sent to Moscow for advanced instruction.

No wonder a spirit of pioneering and optimism pervaded the town, for the exhilaration that comes with taking part in and doing an exciting job was theirs. Weren't they building a metropolis that was to be northern Siberia's Gateway to the World?

Meeting an iceberg in the Kara Sea.

500 STATUTE MILES

NORTH ⊙ POLE

Siberia

Arctic Ocean

Ambarchik

150°E

180°

75°

70°

Wrangel

Markovo

Anadyr

65°

Chuckchee Sea

Beaufort Sea

150°W

120°

Prince Patrick Borden

Bering Strait

60°

Point Hope

★ Tigerak

Pt. Barrow

Bering Sea

Kotzebue

Nootak

Kobuk

Demarcation Point

Banks

Herschel I.

Richard I.

Victoria

Nome

St. Michaels

Yukon

Ft Yukon

Aklavik ★

Fairbanks

Mackenzie

ARCTIC CIRCLE

Dutch Harbor

Bristol Bay

Dawson

Norman Wells

Great Bear Lake

Aleutian Is.

Anchorage

Yukon

Norman

55°

Ft. Simpson

Gulf of Alaska

Skagway

Juneau

50°

Sitka

Richard Edes Harrison
1944

SEVERAL thousand years ago, before any men walked the western hemisphere, that part of Alaska which draws closest to Siberia became the gateway to a new world. The first to come to Alaskan shores were Mongols from Asia, who migrated over a long period of time. Some say there was a land bridge, and that they walked across it, but more likely then, as now, they came in one of man's oldest inventions, the skin boat. These numerous immigrants traveled slowly southeastward into South America, Mexico, the United States and Canada and became our Indians and Eskimos.

Indians and Eskimos, who belong to the same family, for an Eskimo is simply another kind of Indian, became the first settlers of Alaska. In a country a fifth the size of the United States, with every possible climate and terrain, the Eskimos chose the northernmost part to live in. Fishing and hunting, they settled along the Arctic coast, Bering Sea and the interior. Some settled on the river deltas and some on the inland rivers, all living in small communities. They burnt caribou tallow and seal, whale and walrus oil for fuel. They used the skins of the animals that provided them with food for clothing, fashioning them into costumes which kept them as warm as if they had been enclosed in thermos bottles. They heated their practically cold-proof houses to temperatures we associate with Turkish baths, lived a happy life peculiarly well adapted to the country, and thought it the finest in the world.

The coming of the white man changed this picture. First there was disease. Simple diseases like measles and whooping cough, and later influenza, to which the Eskimos had no inherited immunity. They died by the thousands and whole villages were completely wiped out. Then came strange new foods like flour and sugar, which the Eskimos disliked intensely at first, but got used to and finally became dependent upon. With this change in diet their hitherto perfect teeth developed cavities, followed by a frightful thing called toothache which they had never known before. That was on the debit side.

On the credit side were doctors who sometimes cured the new ills the Eskimos were subject to. Men who could set a broken bone so that it would heal and be stronger than ever. Men who could cut out the diseased part of a person who would then recover and be as good as ever. Dentists who pulled and patched teeth. Government schools where young Eskimos were taught to read and write the strange white man's language. Missionaries who brought news of Christianity, converted most of the Eskimos and in many cases looked after and helped their material as well as spiritual welfare. Later there were reindeer which the government provided for the Eskimos to supplement their dwindling food supply and to make them once again independent.

The horrors attending the change from a stone age culture to modern civilization are fading. The Eskimos, and Indians too, are increasing in numbers. They are finding their place in a white man's world, learning trades, becoming teachers and clergymen. They are even taking part in World War II, joining the Army, buying war bonds and collecting money for the Red Cross.

Alaska was little known to most of us before World War II. Some of us knew we bought it from Russia in 1867, that there had been a gold rush round the turn of the century in which men called "sourdoughs" took part, and that the country was big and the population small.

But the war changed all this, bridging the distance between the United States and her little known territory. Suddenly it was no longer remote, for Fairbanks, Dutch Harbor, Anchorage and the Aleutian Islands became household names and Post Office addresses to the families of soldiers stationed at those strategic points. To many of the soldiers it became a new

Food and gear are stored in the family cache, too high for prowling wolves and bears.

found land, a place to bring one's bride and to settle when the war was done. Even General Buckner, Commander of the Alaska Defense Command and a died-in-the-wool Southerner, fell in love with Alaska, purchased land, and now plans to spend the rest of his days in the vast, still comparatively untouched land.

When the Japanese gained possession of several of the Aleutian Islands it was as if all Alaska held its breath, for the country was woefully unprepared. With the attack, the importance of her strategic position, which had been slowly dawning on military and civilian minds alike, now burst like a bomb. There seems little doubt that had the Japanese chosen to follow up their tiny foothold, they might have driven deep into the mainland of the country. Fortunately for all they did not. But not until the last Jap was killed on Attu, the Kiska forces frightened off, and adequate defenses finished, did Alaskans breathe normally again. With grim determination they vowed that never again would they be found unprepared to repel an attack on even the outermost Aleutian Island.

Many people are wont to think of Alaska as an Arctic country, but actually less than one third of its rich lands protrude north of the Circle. The Brooks Range occupies the middle of the area beyond the Circle, and north of it facing the Polar Sea is the low Arctic slope. This is a grassy, flat country, peppered with the usual numberless Arctic lakes and ponds. It lies in the form of a triangle between northwesternmost Alaska, Point Barrow, and Demarcation Point which latter marks the boundary between Alaska and Canada's Yukon. The coast is treeless but inland along the rivers are willows in sufficient numbers to provide fuel and building materials for the Eskimos and whites who live there.

In Arctic Alaska there are no railroads, no automobiles, no roads. At Fort Yukon the great Yukon River curves north of the Circle for a few miles, and here steamboats ply the waters. But for the rest of Alaska's Arctic domain, airplanes, dog teams and Eskimo skin boats are the modes of transportation, with the airplane playing an important and dramatic role. Many Alaskans ride in planes with the same casualness with which we pick up a taxi at a street corner, and Eskimos who have never seen an automobile travel long distances by air.

Airplanes are in the trucking, freighting and taxi business in Alaska. They bring men and machinery to isolated mines, dropping engineers and miners at the opening of the season and picking them up at the close. Fish-

Most of Alaska's Eskimos live along the coasts of Bering Sea, in the Polar Mediterranean and in the river deltas.

ermen who want to get to the fishing grounds before the start of a season, charter a plane, often bringing in heavy equipment with them. Recently all the fishermen, cannery help, and a great deal of equipment was transported to the rich waters of Bristol Bay by air alone. Trappers, too, fly out to their traplines in an hour across terrain that formerly took a week to traverse. Supplies for the season fly along with the trapper and many dog teams have flown thousands of miles and are completely at home in the air.

North of the Circle there are only three towns of any importance in Alaska; Nome, Fairbanks and the other well-known cities are all south of 66° N. Fort Yukon in the interior, is the most historic spot of the three and is famous for its Weather Bureau record of 100° in the shade. Point Hope at the northwestern end of the country is the site of one of the most startling and important archeological finds of the century. Point Barrow, Alaska's farthest north, is most famous in the annals of exploration. More than three hundred miles north of the Circle, this little town has greeted many

An Alaska Eskimo mother with her two children, who do not seem
to enjoy being photographed.

The inverted umiak on stilts, minus its skin cover is a familiar sight in northern Alaska.

famous explorers starting with Captain Beechey in 1826, down to Amundsen, Ellsworth, Nobile, Stefansson and Wilkins in more recent times. No less famous than many of the explorers who have dropped in on him, is Charlie Brower, "king of the Arctic," who has lived at Point Barrow for sixty years, running a trading post, acting as postmaster and magistrate and loving it.

Alaska was discovered centuries ago, but war rediscovered her for us. Just as many gold seekers stayed when the gold rush was over and became Alaskan citizens, so many of our soldiers will stay when the war is finished. Others will return and spread the truth about the weather, resources, and agricultural possibilities of the Territory. Alaska needs settlers. At the start of the war there were about eighty thousand people, half white and half native, living in a country that can easily support ten million. Called the "last frontier," Alaska is also a "land of opportunity" for pioneer-minded persons who can visualize her future in an air age and are willing to build that future.

PREHISTORIC MYSTERY

Tigerak, meaning index finger, is the
appropriate name the Eskimos have for Point Hope, the long, narrow
peninsula with a rounded outer edge, which juts out from Alaska's northwest coast for fifteen miles into the Polar Sea. Close by its flourishing Eskimo village, at a place they named Ipiutak, three young scientists recently
discovered the ruins of an "Arctic metropolis" where a sophisticated, highly
cultured people lived more than twenty centuries ago, in a city larger than
pre-war Fairbanks.

Here, on Tigerak, 130 miles north of the Circle, they found the remains
of a unique settlement about one mile long, laid out in four distinct avenues
which were lined with at least eight hundred houses. Cemeteries were unearthed where hundreds of skeletons, buried in graves of driftwood logs,
were found interred with their finest and most prized possessions. Some of
the buried articles were familiar things, knives, snow goggles, arrowheads
and animal carvings, but others were fantastically elaborate in shape and
design and even experts could not guess their function. Most of the ivory and
bone objects were covered with beautiful designs delicately engraved with
the greatest skill.

But the most startling find of all was the discovery of weird skeletons whose eyes had been gouged out before burial, and ivory eyes with tremendous black jet pupils substituted. What a shock the excavators must have had as they uncovered those staring, unseeing skulls!

Who were the three discoverers? How did they know where to look to find such rich mysteries? Here is the story. In the summer of 1938, among the scientists gathered at Copenhagen for an anthropological congress, were two young men, each of whom had specialized in Eskimo archaeology. Helge Larsen, a tall Danish anthropologist of the National Museum at Copenhagen, had worked among the ancient Eskimo settlements in Greenland, while Froelich B. Rainey, an energetic professor at the University of Alaska, had worked in western Alaska. It was as natural as night following day that the two should seek each other out and compare notes. Soon they were enthusiastically talking of the possibilities of a joint expedition where the Danish knowledge of eastern Eskimo cultures and the American knowledge of western peoples might be mutually helpful in linking the widely separated communities.

Only a few months later Larsen received an invitation from Rainey to take part in just such an expedition to Point Hope, Alaska. He accepted with alacrity and thus the widely separated Royal Danish Museum of Copenhagen, the American Museum of Natural History in New York, and the University of Alaska became joint sponsors of an expedition. Larsen knew Point Hope was one of the most interesting Eskimo settlements in Alaska and offered the largest known collection of ruins in which to dig and delve. In fact another Dane, Knud Rasmussen, had fifteen years before described the village and the extent of the ruins.

In Alaska, Rainey met Larsen and they were joined by a third member, Louis Giddings, also a member of the faculty of the University of Alaska, whose specialty was determining the age of ancient wooden finds by the wood rings. This was of tremendous importance, for heretofore there had been no method of determining exactly the age of Eskimo archaeological finds.

Being modern explorers, the three men arrived by plane at grass-carpeted Point Hope, in July, when millions of brightly colored flowers had splashed patterns against the green. The Eskimos here elect a committee of seven, one of whom acts as mayor, to maintain law and order in the community, and the expedition immediately applied to them for permission to dig. At first the committee was reluctant to give its consent, for it turned out that the natives themselves were all amateur archaeologists, and in summer-

The modern explorer, like almost everyone else in Alaska, travels by airplane.

time, when the seals disappeared from the coast, they dug things up and sold them to traders, or to the crews of the Coast Guard Cutters. They were not interested in competition. Finally an agreement was reached whereby the natives would earn money by helping with the digging and selling food and furs to the white men—so work was begun.

The ruined settlement near the village proved to be not nearly as old as they had expected, so the archaeologists moved further in on the peninsula to a spot called Jabbertown where they found an old settlement which Giddings concluded dated from around the year 1200. It was not, however, extraordinary in any way, being a type that had already been found in Greenland and Canada.

One day a harpoon head was picked up at random. Upon examination it turned out to be extremely old and of a type different from anything the three had seen before. Going back the next day to investigate the spot where it had been picked up, they noticed for the first time faint, quadrangular depressions covered with lush vegetation. They had passed this spot many times before and never noticed anything, but perhaps it was the long slant-

Eskimo family in front of its sod house at Point Hope; the posts in the foreground are jaw bones of the bowhead whale.

ing shadows thrown by the low afternoon sun that had outlined the symmetrical shapes.

Barely able to restrain their excitement, the men, aided by natives, began to dig and to their amazement found that each square outlined the remnants of an ancient house. Inside they found artifacts which were older than anything that had ever been found in the Arctic. And they were different, too. Exceptionally fine flints, long and wafer-thin, were found. Eskimos had never had such tools. Elaborate, delicately-carved designs, covered the ivory and bone implements. These people were not Eskimos! Or were they? What had the explorers unearthed?

In the short three weeks left to them before the Coast Guard Cutter was to pick them up, Rainey, Larsen and Giddings worked feverishly to answer some of those questions. They were able to excavate nine of the scores of houses, and they collected more than a thousand artifacts. As Larsen said, they had found the treasure trove, and had lifted the lid slightly. Promising to come back the next year to continue the digging, the men took leave of

The primitive bow drill is still used by a few Eskimos. This one is making a fish lure of walrus ivory.

Dr. Helge Larsen, one of the three who discovered Ipiutak.

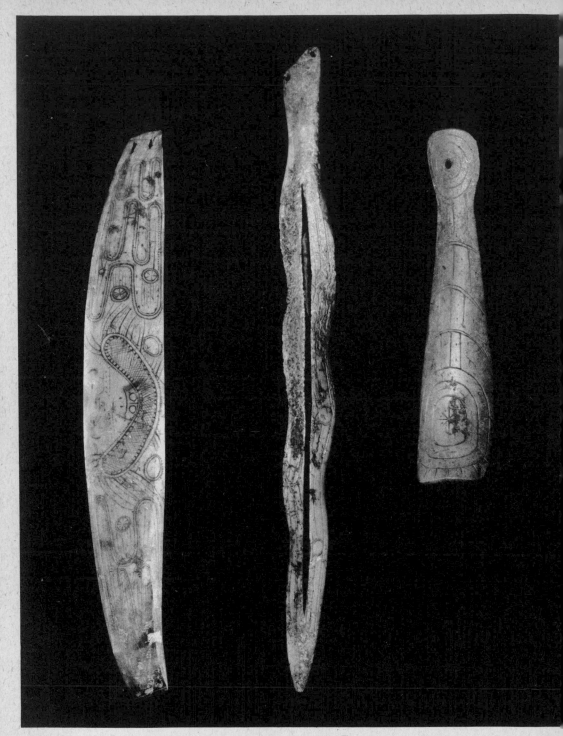

These are artifacts to the scientists, primitive utensils, or carvings to us. Can you guess their function? The piece on the right that looks like a shoehorn is probably a bowman's wrist guard; the center article may be a harpoon head; the beautifully carved object facing out is probably a bag handle.

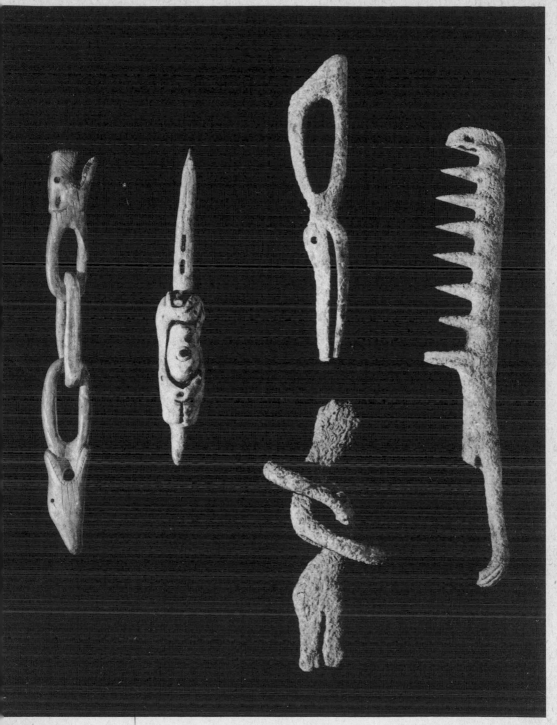

Everything on both these pages is made of ivory. No one knows what the strange articles on this page were used for. The two-piece affair nearest the bottom will come apart, like some of our metal ring puzzles. Was this a child's toy?

(above) One of the mystery people of Ipiutak carved this ivory beast. (below) The use of
the two lower pieces is unknown; the lowest one might be a decorative caribou head.

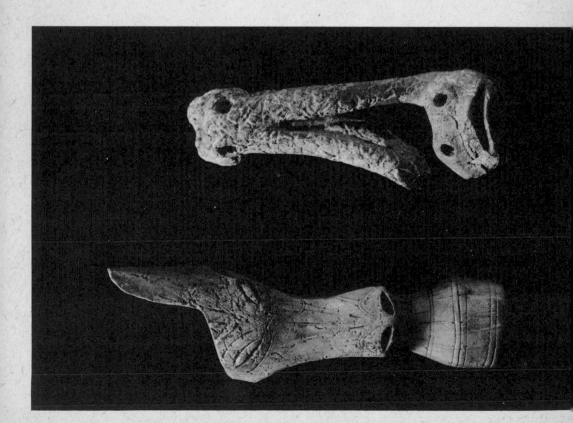

Large ivory eyes, with huge, staring jet pupils, greeted the archaeologists who uncovered this skeleton of Ipiutak man.

the ribbon-like spit of Tigerak, and the ancient town which they named Ipiutak.

But in April, 1940, the Germans invaded Denmark and Larsen was unable to leave the country. Rainey, however, returned in January of that year to live with the Point Hope Eskimos. He hunted the bowhead whale with them, took part in their celebrations, gaining insight into the customs of the living Eskimos in order to enlarge his understanding of their ancestors. In spring he was joined by a student from the University of Alaska, and it was only then, by a strange circumstance, that the full extent of the settlement was discovered.

Grass and moss on western Point Hope began to turn green in June while the slightly higher grass covering the house sites still retained the yellowish cast of dead grass from the season before. Thus the outline of each house stood out sharp and clear, and it was seen that the settlement was laid out in four long rows, which the men called First to Fourth Avenues. As they began to count, their amazement grew, for they counted more than six hundred houses! Later, two hundred more houses were found on the shore, buried beneath the sand. Others, they suspected, had been carried off by the ocean, which is gradually eating away the northern and western shores of Point Hope. This, then, must have been a city of a thousand houses, where as many as three thousand people had dwelt, a city greater than modern Fairbanks, the metropolis of present-day Alaska! Nothing comparable to this had ever been found in any part of the Arctic. A settlement of a few hundred souls had previously been considered about the limit for an Arctic community.

No skeletons were found in the houses and, knowing they could not be far off, Rainey instituted a systematic search which at first yielded no results. Finally he recruited every available man, woman and child in the village to help with the work. After digging hundreds of test pits over a wide area, the graves were found and with them the richest, most elaborate implements, which had been buried with the bodies. There were also the beautiful nameless objects the experts are still puzzled about, some spiral shaped, others twisted like pretzels. Besides the ivory eyes mentioned before, some of the skulls had ivory cup-shaped mouth covers, and in one case ivory nose plugs carved in the form of birds and set with jet eyes. The fantastic appearance of one skull is shown on page 117. The skull of a loon was found in one grave, and it, too, had ivory and jet eyes. No doubt the loon had some symbolic significance but its exact nature we shall probably never know.

The decorative designs which embellish the Ipiutak articles are different from most Eskimo designs. Oriental is the guess of most people who examine them, but Oriental experts have been called in to examine the cunningly made objects and none have found their parallel in Oriental art. Who were these people? They were undoubtedly Asiatic, but from whence did they come? Why did they migrate? What became of them?

Helge Larsen, one of the trio who discovered Ipiutak, believes that these people gradually adopted Eskimo ways, as they found them better suited to the climate and terrain. He thinks the 250 Eskimos living today at Point Hope are the direct descendents of the mysterious persons who made up the largest and most ancient Eskimo settlement in the world.

The average Eskimo community is small; few indeed number more than two hundred. How then was this Arctic country able to support a city of thousands? The bowhead whale and the walrus might well be the answer to that question. The whale is so large it can feed an average village for weeks. The heavily-built walrus, ten or eleven feet long, travels in herds and these animals are so fat they could considerably augment any food supply. Then, too, the prehistoric city of Ipiutak flourished long before the reckless near-extermination of oil-bearing animals. Point Hope lies directly in the path of the yearly northward migration of whales and walrus to the Arctic Sea which still takes place between April and June. Before their terrible depletion the schools of whale and the herds of walrus that passed by must have been so large as to stagger the imagination.

Although their descendants soon afterwards learned the trick, there is little evidence to show that Ipiutak people lived by whaling. Their frail bird spears and delicate arrowheads could never have killed a whale, and few harpoon heads were found. They did live on walrus, and hunted the ordinary hair seal and the large bearded seal. Caribou, too, formed part of their diet, for remnants of all these animals were found in refuse heaps.

The abundance of arrowheads, the comparatively few harpoons and the absence of the typical Eskimo-type implements suggest to Rainey that the residents of Ipiutak were formerly an inland people dependent normally on land game, who came to the coast only for the seasonal hunting of sea mammals. This might be one explanation, for it was true in the boom whaling days when hundreds of Eskimos from north and south would settle at Point Hope during the season to take part in the hunt and in the tremendous celebration that always followed (and still does) the capture of the whales. But it might be equally true that if the numbers of whales and walrus captured were great enough they could have supported the settlement all year round, especially if the smaller animals were hunted as well.

What kind of animal is the bowhead whale which might have supported Ipiutak and which the Point Hope village depends on today for survival? It belongs to a family of the mightiest mammals on earth. Its cousin the Blue Whale is not only the largest animal in the world but it is said to surpass in size and weight the largest dinosaurs that ever roamed the earth. The velvety black bowhead is next in size, averaging between fifty and sixty-five feet in length and, unlike some of its relations, having no teeth. Instead, it is equipped with long, narrow strips of baleen or "whalebone" which hang from either edge of its upper jaws. These blades become longer toward the middle of each row, sometimes attaining almost 12 feet, and narrowing down to a few inches at the ends. This was the material so highly prized for stiffening ladies' corsets, for bustles, hoopskirts and high stiff collars, which brought more than four dollars per pound near the end of the last century.

The bowhead has two blowholes and, like all whales, must come up to the surface of the water to breathe every five or ten minutes, although they have been known to remain below for as long as forty-five minutes. The young are about fifteen feet long when born, and are suckled by their mothers for about a year on milk not very different from cow's milk. Mother and child are most affectionate, and if one is killed, the other will not leave its side, and becomes easy prey for the hunter.

Despite long contact with white men, the coming of spring and the whaling season brings out among the modern Eskimos many of the old beliefs, legends and customs which are strangely mingled with the newer religion of Christianity. Hunters formerly used chants and charms to compel the lady in the moon to help in securing whales; now prayer is addressed to Jehovah. Songs and dances, feasts and prayers are the prelude to the great activity of preparation. Strict rules govern all the phases of preparation as well as the actual hunt.

The gear used in the hunt must be clean and, if possible, new, for tradition says that if the whale sees shiny bright gear it pleases him, for it

Peter Kunukuoruk, the chief whaler of Point Hope. He is wearing a translucent, waterproof coat made from seal or Walrus intestines.

One man holds the whale with a boat hook while another starts the cutting operations with his keen-edged spade.

means the knives will be sharp and will not hurt when he is butchered. Rainey tells that the Eskimos believe the whale does not die, he only "has his coat removed," and if it is done painlessly he returns to the sea and reports favorably on his treatment to his fellow whales.

For the same reason as their ancestors, the present-day Eskimos regard Tigerak as an ideal site for a settlement, and so it is. Extending, as it does, far out into the ocean, there is always a ready supply of food handy for those skillful enough to get it. These Eskimos are skillful; they have to be. Catching a bowhead whale from a small skin boat is dangerous and exciting work. A single false move at the climax may mean disaster and death, for smashing the delicate craft and drowning its crew is child's play for a whale, which can manage it with a single slap of his mighty tail if given the chance.

In spring, when the ice begins to break up, it is the wind that determines when the landfast, or shore, ice shall separate from the moving pack beyond, leaving a dark lane of open water between. This water lane, called a lead, may vary in width from yards to miles and is usually opened by a northeaster and closed by a southwester. The migrating whales travel

This small bowhead whale, thirty to forty feet long, is being killed with a lance after it has been harpooned several times.

through these leads on their way to the cooler waters of the Polar Sea where they find a greater abundance of crustaceans on which to feed than in warmer tropical waters, which they visit each year so that baby whales may be born in comfort.

As soon as the lead opens, all the whaling gear, extra clothing, guns and food necessary for an extended bivouac are loaded into a skin boat, called umiak, which is then dragged along the snow, or pulled on a low boat sled to the edge of the landfast ice. Here, while the sight of a whale is awaited, the time is spent telling stories, making the ingenious Eskimo string figures which are an incredibly complicated version of our "cat's cradle," discussing topics of the day or just waiting. During all this time the men are without tents, sleeping bags or shelter of any kind, except for an ice windbreak. Formerly no cooking was allowed on the ice, wet clothing could not be changed, and even an iceblock windbreak was prohibited. The old men shake their heads and consider the younger generation soft, for they have hot tea and food, and dry clothes to change into. The cycle of waiting and hunting continues until a southwester closes the lead; when it opens the process begins all over again.

Dr. Froelich B. Rainey (center, or third from right) and his Point Hope
whaling companions.

When a whale is killed, each boat that is in the vicinity at the time receives a share of it, but the amount depends on the order of its arrival at
the kill. The second boat to arrive gets a large share, while the last gets a
kind of "booby" prize. All paddlers strain every muscle as they hear the
shout "argverk"—"whale!" When it is killed the boat which first sighted
it takes the lead in towing it back to shore. Rainey tells us that as they
start back someone shouts "a short repeated barking sound, like the cry of
a sea lion," and he is soon joined by the others making a noisy din as they
move shoreward. This is a signal to the cooks who remain on the ice edge.
They then relay word to the village that the first whale of spring has been
killed.

As the whale is cut up and divided, dog teams race back and forth from
the ice to underground storage pits ashore, hauling the tons of fresh meat.
Every scrap of the whale, including the heart, intestine, lungs, baleen and
bone are used. Everything, that is, except the bare skull which is returned

Preparing to re-cover the umiak used in the whale hunt.

Two Eskimo women dance at the whale feast to the accompaniment of drums and singing.

to the sea, no one now remembers why, but that is what has been done since the eldest villager can remember. Whalebone replaces wood for almost every purpose in the village. Even the huge jawbones are used and become monuments at the feasting grounds, or door frames and fenceposts, and the village cemetery is surrounded by a neat picket fence made of whale ribs.

In June, the day after the boats return from the ice and whaling is over for the year, busy preparations begin for *Nalukataktut,* the feasting time. Women sew new clothes for the occasion and talk of little else for days ahead. Great quantities of whale meat are consumed. Many sorts of contests are held, and there is much singing and dancing to the accompaniment of drums.

The high spot of the festival, which sometimes lasts three days, is the blanket tossing game called *Nalukataktut,* from which the holiday gets its name. A large walrus hide is grasped by forty or fifty people who then dare some courageous celebrator to climb up on it. The brave one then finds himself tossed ten or fifteen feet in the air and tries to remain upright and land on his feet each time. An inexpert "dancer in the air" is at the mercy of the tossers and falls on his back and sprawls in ridiculous poses which he is unable to control, to the delight of the audience. Real experts

Colored glasses are worn to protect the eyes from the white glare that causes snowblindness.

Eskimos formerly made snow goggles of wood, with narrow slits, to let in a minimum of light; now most of them use sun glasses of the type we can buy in the corner drug store.

are able to keep time with their arms, body and legs to the singing and drumming which are kept up during the game. *Nalukataktut,* which combines a delicious kind of terror with thrilling gaiety, was formerly performed only once a year at the whaling feast; now it has become a part of many hilarious Eskimo celebrations in other Alaskan villages, especially on the Fourth of July.

When the missionaries came to Point Hope, the power of the medicineman, or *shaman,* gradually waned and soon disappeared. Today all the Eskimos are good Christians and attend the Episcopal church twice every Sunday. But many of the old beliefs survive, especially in the whaling hunts, and some taboos are still observed although more quietly than formerly and sometimes in secret.

Like other Alaskan Eskimo villages, Point Hope has reindeer, part of the original herd distributed by the U. S. Government to augment the food supply of the Eskimos. In 1939 there were 3500 deer at the village and they were managed by a cooperative reindeer company run by the natives. These deer are an insurance against famine, and the surplus provides skins for clothing and meat for food.

There is also a cooperative trading store at Tigerak which sells furs, brought in from the interior by the Eskimos, to buyers in the United States. With the proceeds, imported necessities are purchased for the members. The store was started in 1920 by thirteen Eskimos, and today most of the male members of the community own stock.

There is a government school where the children are taught to read and write in English. The town has a good landing field for airplanes, which is easily accessible from Fairbanks, Nome and Kotzebue.

Ipiutak has been made a National Monument and protected from casual digging by tourists and others. By a happy stroke of luck, Larsen was able to leave Denmark with his family and is now at the American Museum of Natural History in New York. Here he is sorting, comparing and collating the more than ten thousand Ipiutak specimens of ivory, bone and flint, remnants of another age. Soon he will publish, with Rainey, the results of the expedition wherein many startling revelations may await us. From now on all archaeologists will be on the lookout for traces of Ipiutak culture in other regions, and perhaps one day we will really know the answer to the riddle of the mysterious first settlers of Alaska.

CANADA'S domain north of the Circle is second largest in the world. A broad strip of woods and prairie stretches eastward from Alaska to Foxe Basin; the rest is "Canada's Arctic Islands" which are the bane of cartographers, for there are so many of them, they are of every imaginable size and shape, and intricate, irregular straits and passages separate them. They stretch from below the Circle almost as far northward as Greenland's northernmost tip. Some of them are mountainous, like eastern Baffin and Ellesmere, parts of which are covered with permanent snow and ice; others are low, and grassy in summer. Some of them are uninhabited, others have trading posts, small Eskimo settlements, and perhaps a Royal Canadian Mounted Police post.

Victoria, Banks, Melville, Prince Patrick, King William, Somerset, Borden —these are only a few of the islands whose very names conjure up colorful pictures of romance and adventure. Each island has its own peculiar story. Who was the first to find it? Who mapped it? After whom was it named, and why? Who lost his life in attempting to reach it? What new facts or laws of science were discovered here?

Each island has a role in the pageant of exploration. Death and defeat, as well as fame, reward and success, take important parts in the drama.

Scurvy and frostbite are two of the worst villains, and the mighty ice pack, most powerful force of all in the High North, plays a dual role. Sometimes it moves to crush a sturdily built ship, sometimes to open a lead rich with game that yields food, fuel and clothing to the skillful hunter. It may block the progress of a fleet, but it may also bridge the sea between island and mainland so that an army could march across.

Most of these islands were found during the search for the Northwest Passage; that quest which captured the imagination of men's minds from the time of John Cabot to the end of the last century. The passage was found at the cost of incredible hardship and tragedy, and when at last it was discovered it went practically unused. Perhaps with the northward movement of men and industry, and the help of weather and ice reporting, it will be now used to join the waters of the Atlantic and Pacific Oceans.

"Canada Moves North," says the title of Richard Finnie's book. The big industries haven't quite reached the Circle, but they are on their way. The oil from rich Fort Norman fields is not very far south, and its abundance is already being piped to Whitehorse and Fairbanks in Alaska. The Alaska Highway or Alcan, is south of the Circle but it leads northward. On Great Bear Lake, still farther north, radium was discovered and is being mined. Gold, copper, quartz and other rich minerals are there waiting for strong hands and pioneer minds to develop them. The population of Arctic Canada has always been too sparse, handfuls of people sprinkled across vast distances, but activities like the Canol project and the highway help to increase it, for some people always stay on when the work is finished.

Aviation is changing the picture here, too. Canadians are said to carry more freight per capita by air than any other people and the North Country is responsible. For lack of railroads and highways, whole mining plants have been flown into remote settlements, unassembled smokestacks, even grand pianos have made aerial trips. Radium concentrates fly back from Port Radium, furs fly back from Aklavik and other fur trading centers, mine operators, traders and geologists fly in and out on their various businesses. Doctors, policemen, missionaries fly throughout the Canadian North.

The story of the finding of radium, the world's most precious element, on the shores of Great Bear Lake, is as startling and romantic as anything in fiction. Although the spot is thirty odd miles south of the Circle it is indicative of the kind of activity that is moving northward.

A prospector named Gilbert La Bine was poring over some early Cana-

This is a modern Canadian Eskimo family. Notice the sewing machine at the left, the portable phonograph, and the iron stove.

dian Government geological reports when he encountered references to cobalt bloom on rocks found thirty years before by Camsell and Bell. La Bine was looking for silver and the presence of cobalt spelt silver to him. So, in the spring of 1930, with a companion, he was dropped by plane into the hills around Great Bear Lake (the largest in Canada), where the cobalt had been reported. As they were working their way to what is known today as Echo Bay, La Bine's friend became snowblind. While he was resting, La Bine carried on some prospecting of his own and found the cobalt stained ore, and the silver, but he also discovered a blackish piece of pitchblende. Now pitchblende is the richest known source of radium, and one can imagine with what excitement La Bine sent the specimen off to Ottawa and awaited the analysis. The ore was found to be very rich in radium, that fabulous and rare substance discovered by Eve Curie and her husband, which is used among other things today in the treatment of cancer.

At the time of the discovery Belgians had a tight monopoly on the radium business and were said to be the only producers. Pitchblende in quantity was found only in Czechoslovakia and the Belgian Congo and the market price per gram was $70,000. The rich Canadian sources reduced the price to $25,000 and $30,000 per gram, making it available to more hospitals all over the world. The open-handed Canadian policy dispelled the veil of secrecy which had heretofore surrounded the production of radium, by publicly announcing the yield of the mines and the prices—very different from the Belgian policy which was secret and fostered all sorts of spy stories and tales of secret formulas.

Perhaps the greatest role the Canadian Arctic will play is in long range aviation. Get out your globe again and see that most of the great air routes of the world will have to cross Canada at one place or another. Seattle to London, San Francisco to Leningrad, New York to Chungking, Chicago to Calcutta, all lead across the Canadian Arctic. The world of the future will see modern airports scattered throughout the Canadian Arctic.

DAIRY FARMING BY THE POLAR SEA

WHEN Charles and Anne Lindbergh, flying "north to the Orient," set their orange-winged ship *Sirius* down at the little town of Aklavik, in August, 1931, many people in the United States read and pronounced the strange name for the first time. For a moment the whole world's attention was focused on this Arctic hamlet, and its aviation possibilities pondered. Most of us thought it curious, then, that the famous couple should fly from Ottawa to China by way of northernmost Canada and Alaska—but "great circle course" had not yet become one of our everyday phrases.

Aklavik (Eskimo for "place of bears") lies on the mighty Mackenzie River, about sixty miles from its wide mouth. Here the impatient river, as though sensing its nearness to journey's end, is no longer content with a single channel, but splits and spills into numerous new paths that intertwine and cross each other like some huge spider-web or maze. Hundreds of large and small islands, peppered with spruce-fringed lakes, crowd the delta. Although Aklavik is more than a hundred miles north of the Circle and has the honor of being the most northerly settlement on the Canadian mainland, spruce trees reach heights of fifty and sixty feet. Larch and willow, too, line the river banks, adding their color to the rich green of the summer landscape, surprising the tourists who come for a glimpse of the "barren North."

The Lindbergh visit was not the opening gun of aviation's advance northward toward the Arctic Sea. The start was made six years earlier when the Government established a weather and radio station at Aklavik, one of a series which now number a dozen, spread across the width of the Arctic as far east as Hudson Strait. Several times a day temperatures, barometric pressure, wind direction and velocity are radioed to the Canadian Meteorological Service where the figures and degree signs, which mean safety to flyers throughout Canada, are recorded and collated.

Accurate information about weather is one of the most important sinews of flight. Without it an aviator is as handicapped as a musician with only one good ear, or a dancer with one leg. Knowledge of the weather's pets and tantrums is as essential to uninterrupted schedules as smooth-running engines and adequate fuel. The Canadian Arctic stations are filling in the blank areas on the weather maps, thus aiding the forecasting of storms throughout the rest of North America. The stations also handle commercial radio messages, linking the people of Aklavik with their friends, relatives and business associates "outside." From 1925 on, the use of radio and plane in the North increased by leaps and bounds, and was climaxed on July 1, 1929, when "Punch" Dickens, one of Canada's great aerial pioneers, brought his monoplane to rest on the delta of the Mackenzie—the very first to come down at Aklavik.

What was the reaction of the local Eskimos, who had never seen a plane before, to this miraculous sight? Richard Finnie, in his excellent book *Canada Moves North,* tells of the wise old Eskimo woman who witnessed the event and flatly stated: "I don't believe it—the wings don't flap." A Coronation Gulf Eskimo having the same experience admitted: "It's a big bird all right, but I doubt there is much meat on it."

One thing we can be fairly sure of is that not much time would be lost before the mechanically ingenious Eskimos would carefully examine the ship, politely ask for rides, and try to figure out what makes it go. Their interest in mechanical things is not a newly acquired trait, the gift of "civiliza-

The tattoo mark on Lucy Carpenter's chin dates her, for now only the older people have them.

tion." From earliest days explorers have told of the remarkable skill with which an Eskimo could invent, build and repair all sorts of mechanical devices. One has been known to fix the first outboard motor he had ever seen. Another had a dollar watch which stopped after a year or two of service. Although he had never seen the inside of a watch before, he took it apart, cleaned, oiled and put it together again—and it ran!

Today freight as well as passengers come to Aklavik throughout the year by transport plane. Canadian Pacific Airlines maintains its schedule, landing on pontoons in summer and switching to skis in winter. Besides mail, anything from cattle to mining machinery may come in by plane, while outgoing freight consists mostly of white fox furs.

When a mail plane is due, children playing outdoors are usually the first to spot it and run home as fast as their little legs will take them, screaming: "Airplane coming—airplane coming!" The mail-bag is dumped and sorted in the midst of an excited group and little can be accomplished in the way of school work, housework, in fact, work of any kind, until the precious letters and packets have been distributed. Squeals of delight are heard as packages are opened, sighs of frustration if the wrong item has been sent, and there is quiet disappointment if an expected package fails to materialize.

For twenty-four hours after the landing of a mail plane, practically no one, except perhaps babies, gets any sleep. Everyone is busy reading letters and hastily writing answers for the waiting plane to carry out. Formerly there was no mail delivery for three months after the freeze-up. Planes had to wait for freeze-up just north of Edmonton in order to take off there on skis. But in 1943 planes landed on wheels at Norman Wells, scene of the great oil development, about 300 miles southeastward of Aklavik. Here they changed to skis for landing at the more northerly village and mail came throughout the winter for the first time.

Aklavik played a dramatic part in Sir Hubert Wilkins's extraordinary search for the lost Soviet flyers in 1937. On August 12 of that year a four-motored plane left Moscow heading for Fairbanks, Alaska, by way of the North Pole. Its crew of six was led by one of the Soviet Union's most beloved heroes, Sigismund Levanevsky, and about half of them had had previous Arctic experience. Flying steadily along the Fairbanks meridian, the plane was two hours flying time past the North Pole when a radio message announced that one of the motors had gone dead, and that ice was forming on the plane. The last intelligible words, "We are landing in . . . " were followed by garbled signals and then—silence.

Through the Explorers Club in New York, a rescue expedition, headed by Sir Hubert Wilkins, was quickly organized, and less than ten days after the flyers were overdue long flights over the Polar Sea were in progress. Aklavik was the main base of operations and flights continued until March of the following year.

The lost flyers were never found, but in the course of the search Wilkins made great contributions to Arctic flying. About 170,000 square miles of the Polar Sea were flown over and explored, of which an area larger than Montana had never before been sighted by man. The first Polar Sea flights by moonlight in history were made, and a distance of 44,000 miles flown. The moonlight flights were perhaps the most important result, for they exploded still one more "bogie" in the folklore of the High North.

Most of us are familiar with the Far North's continuous sunlight in midsummer; the all-day moon in midwinter is less well known, but Wilkins knew it and used it to the greatest advantage during the search. If you were on the southern edge of the Arctic during December, January and February, you would see the full moon never setting, instead circling continuously for one, two or three consecutive days and nights. As you moved northward the period would lengthen until you were at the North Pole, where you would have continuous moonlight for about fifteen out of each twenty-eight days. Here the moon would rise before it was half size, remaining in the sky through full and a little after half again.

The pitch black night of the Polar Regions that lasts six months, is just a myth like Santa Claus. Down north in winter when, during much of the day, there is no direct or indirect sunlight, the sparkling white, snow-covered ground so reflects and magnifies whatever light reaches it, that even at the darkest period you can probably see a darkly-clad man against a white background a hundred yards away. For even when the sky is overcast and there is neither twilight nor moon, and no northern lights illumine the sky, the stars alone succeed in transmitting enough light through the densest clouds so that when it is reflected by the snow it prevents the type of pitch darkness with which we are familiar in non-polar zones. Only in an open sea that has no ice at all (like that to the north and northeast of Iceland) will you ever encounter pitch darkness inside either of the polar circles.

Wilkins found that with a three-quarters moon, planes could make emergency landings and take-offs as efficiently as by daylight. Some flyers think bright moonlight is even better than daylight, for there is no glare, shadows are remarkably clear cut, and it is easier to distinguish between rough and smooth ice. The *aurora borealis,* or northern lights, which may give as much light as a full moon, are also an aid to the northern flyer.

During a time when there were six or seven hours of twilight each day, Sir Hubert often took off from Aklavik several hours before dawn. By the time light reached Aklavik he had flown far north to latitudes where there is no daylight in midwinter. Turning back when his fuel supply was low, he would return to his base after twilight so that throughout the flight he would never see daylight.

Aklavik's "plat du jour," as one writer put it, is reindeer meat. Indistinguishable from beef, according to some epicures, far better according to others—all agree it is delicious food. The town gets its reindeer from Richards Island, about fifty miles northeast, on the shores of the Beaufort Sea, where the Canadian Government has established a reindeer station. Intended to bring a new means of livelihood to the Eskimos, and to supplement their food supply, the use of domesticated deer also conserves the Territory's diminishing wild life.

With great foresight, the Government decided to import three thousand reindeer from Alaska which would form the nucleus of a great herd, for reindeer will double in numbers every three years if protected from wolves. The story of the long migration, which covered more than fifteen hundred miles of difficult terrain, is as dramatic and exciting as any tale of fiction. The trek, in charge of Andrew Bahr, an experienced Lapp herder, took five years to complete from 1929 to 1935 and survived attacks of mosquitoes, storms in which the herds were scattered. The homing instinct of the deer impelled them to head for home at every opportunity, but especially when surprised or frightened. When the herd finally arrived at the Government corrals only one-fifth of the original number were left. Blizzards, starvation and wolves accounted for this great loss, but the missing four-fifths was almost entirely replaced by the young animals born during the migration. Since then the herds of reindeer (the same animal as caribou except that it is domestic) have increased under the careful supervision of Eskimo youths trained by Lapp experts. In 1943 they numbered twelve thousand. The surplus deer supply Aklavik and neighboring towns with fresh meat and the skins are made into the warmest clothing known to man.

About 350 miles northeastward of Aklavik, far from the mainland of

Baling and sorting Aklavik's feathery "white gold." White fox skins are prepared for shipping at the Hudson's Bay Company post.

Canada, is an island about the size of Vermont and New Hampshire, which
houses about a dozen of the richest Eskimo families in the North. Banks
Island is the westernmost of the Canadian Arctic archipelago, and is part
of the reserve the Government has set aside for its Indians and Eskimos.
No white man may set a trap or kill a living thing here, and these few
Eskimo families have the vast, grassy island to themselves.

Eleven months of each year they spend more than three hundred miles
north of the Circle, hunting and trapping, but late each summer they arrive
at Aklavik to trade their winter's catch of white fox and polar bear. They
come in excellent ships loaded to the gunwales with dogs, children and
skins. One of their ships is the famous *North Star,* which played such a
dramatic role in Stefansson's Canadian Arctic Expedition of 1913-18. Three
families together own the boat which they purchased for $25,000. It takes
a great many white fox skins to make up that amount, but Banks Island,
so rich in animal life, is able to supply them. Other families have equally
good ships, the *Nanook,* the *Omingmuk,* tidy schooners with shining
engines and scrupulously clean interiors. One of them even has a red and
white color scheme carefully carried out in the galley. The men smoke

139

Hair seals brought in by these two Eskimos will be used for dog feed. Large ones will sell for $8.00, small ones $4.00.

cigars. These families pay income taxes up to $10,000, which are collected by the R.C.M.P. Inspector.

During their yearly visit the downy, white furs are turned first into cash, and then into sewing machines, guns, gasoline, canned goods and yard goods. Candy and fresh oranges are especially sought after—all to the tune of much good natured visiting and joking. Their favorite Aklavik trading post is Peffers, and therein lies another story which we will tell later.

The Banks Islanders usually time their annual visit to coincide with the arrival of one of the Hudson's Bay Company's paddle-wheeled steamers. In normal times this happened three times a season, and then "shiptime"

School children crowd around crate with three goats, the first they have ever seen, for a farmer just outside Aklavik. The famous "S.S. Mackenzie River," is in the background.

might well be a synonym for holiday time. The famous *Mackenzie River* or one of her sister ships, would thrash the calm river waters into a white foam as she steamed down to Aklavik, propelled by her log-burning engines. In the old days stops would be made along the tree-studded river banks while four-foot logs were cut to feed the hungry furnaces, but now neat piles of logs are usually waiting along the way. Several live steers and a few hogs and sheep are carried aboard to supply the ship's restaurant, and, while the steamer is loading and unloading, a good portion of the population, many of whom have been living on canned goods most of the year, troop aboard for a meal of fresh meat.

Barge loaded with gasoline drums. Barges are numbered according to capacity; No. 101 can carry 100 tons of freight.

One of the contributory causes of boat-time excitement is the celebration of a kind of Field Day featuring a tug-of-war between Indian and Eskimo women, with races and contests for all. There are hot dogs and ice cream, and the proceeds, which may total as much as $500, are usually donated to the Red Cross.

Enormous tonnages of freight are borne down the river each year on barges which are lashed to the bow and sides of the steamers. Sometimes as many as five are handled by a single boat, but the more barges a steamer pushes and pulls, the more delicate the job of navigating her through the shallow winding parts of the journey. Unlike river captains on the more

Margaret Stewart, an old Indian woman, knits for the Red Cross.

Natkusiak, or Billy Banksland, a famous Canadian Eskimo hunter was a member of Stefansson's second and third expeditions. He is shown with Topsy, his wife, their two children, and Molly Goose and her baby.

peaceful Mississippi, Mackenzie River skippers have a great many natural handicaps to contend with.

The dull red barges are like floating warehouses. Everything from soap and syrup to livestock and ore-crushing machinery is carefully stowed and made secure. Chemicals and dynamite for the mines require the same delicate handling as radio sets and crates of eggs. The barges are numbered. Number 250 indicates that it can carry 250 tons of freight, Number 101, means a "hundred tonner" and so on up to the giant Number 500, which can transport up to six hundred tons of freight without difficulty.

River freighting is slow compared with air express, but it is also very much cheaper, and a great deal more merchandise can be delivered at each trip. When a boat arrives, the depleted stocks of the village stores are replenished and the shelves are once more crowded with attractive merchandise. Aklavik's population of 167 whites and about 700 Eskimos and Indians, know that they can get the best selections at or soon after boat time. They come in from the town's environs to trade, and the streets and shops are crowded and noisy with their chattering, joking and bargaining.

144

Some years ago a man named Henry Peffer cut a large load of spruce on the Mackenzie River. When he could not get what he considered a fair price for the lumber, he fashioned the logs into a raft, built a small log house atop it, and floated all down the Mackenzie to Aklavik. Here, equipped with a store of trade goods and a span of horses, he moved his log house ashore, built a trading post of the raft logs, and opened shop. He prospered and the post grew. The original log cabin store is now a combination movie house, restaurant and store house, while a newer and larger building of finished lumber with large glass windows has taken its place.

Peffer shows sixteen millimeter prints of old movies, and charges one dollar for the privilege of viewing the show. Many of the wealthier Eskimos are content to see the same picture again and again, and one wonders what fun they get out of some of our Hollywood efforts. Eliot Elisofon, a Life Magazine photographer, tells of going to Peffer's to see Hugh Herbert in *Little Accident*. One scene in the movie shows the "little accident," not yet old enough to talk, being asked first "Parlez-vous Francais?" When there was no answer, he was asked the same question in German, then Spanish, and finally the interrogator shrugged his shoulders and said: "Probably an Eskimo." There wasn't a murmur from the well behaved Eskimos, some of whom speak English as well as their own language.

Peffer's largest storage room also serves as a dance hall on special occasions when Eskimo dances are held. The room is cleared and packing boxes become the equivalent of gilt chairs, while native drums and a choir of singing Eskimo women provide the orchestral accompaniment for the dancing, which lasts far into the night.

One of the most hopeful features of Canada's North country, to the believers in a "Friendly Arctic," is the Polar Sea Dairy Farm at Aklavik. Here, almost at the edge of the "Frozen Sea," Dr. Leslie David Livingstone, without mumbo-jumbo or trickery has brought forth upon the frozen subsoil abundant green things, and from small beginnings has raised the most northerly herd of cattle in North America, which supplies the children of the town with fresh milk.

This amiable Scotsman, an Arctic veteran, has as many titles as Pooh-bah in the Mikado. His main job is that of Government doctor, but he is also Indian Agent, Agent of Eskimo Affairs, Justice of the Peace, supervisor of the curriculum of the Mission Schools, and pharmacist. With his wife, he came north to Aklavik in 1938, and decided to try his hand at stock raising and farming, as a hobby. By 1943 he had built, at his own expense, a large modern barn, with room for twenty cattle, and with the help of local labor had cleared forty acres of land, twenty-five of which are good pasture. A tractor delivered in 1941 has aided greatly in increasing the acreage under cultivation. Local wild hay and two fields of barley and oats do not supply quite enough fodder for the herd, and the doctor imports about two tons of feed a year, but he is hopeful that this practice will be discontinued as the extent of his cultivated land increases.

Fresh beef is scarce at a faraway place like Aklavik, and quickly disappears. When an animal from the Livingstone herd of thirteen is killed, the Livingstone table is heavy with large beef roasts, and an invitation to dine is a treat. Besides choice beef, the table will likely offer home grown cauliflower or broccoli, potatoes, pickled beets, and lettuce and cabbage salad. Sweet fresh butter, buttermilk and even ice cream grace their board, shocking those visitors who expect families as far north as the Livingstones to subsist on a diet of hard tack and seal blubber.

Raw milk, whose bottle caps read "Polar Sea Dairy Farm," is sold at twenty-five cents a quart. In cold weather some of it is poured into shallow pans and allowed to freeze. It can then be stored in blocks and thawed out as needed. In this way children of remote trappers as well as the doctor's neighbors may have fresh milk over a period of time.

Following the example of the Roman Catholic Missionaries who have a subterranean storage chamber two storeys deep, the Livingstones have their own cold storage plant, dug fourteen feet down into the frozen sub-soil or perma-frost. Here meat can be kept preserved indefinitely, summer and winter alike. Richard Finnie tells us that while the storage chambers seem to be cold enough to keep meat frozen throughout the year, they are not cold enough in summer to freeze it in the first place. The Catholic Mission now has an imported "quick-freezing" unit where food is chilled, and then transferred to the underground chambers for safe keeping.

While the Livingstones are perhaps the most enterprising farmers at Aklavik, many of the other residents have excellent gardens, and during the comparatively short growing season of twelve weeks raise a good part of their daily fare. Twenty-four-hour-a-day sunlight is the main reason for the rapid growth of the remarkably fine vegetable crops. For plants grow not according to how many days old they are but the number of hours of sunlight they absorb. The constant sun gradually thaws more and more

Dr. Livingstone milking Belinda, first cow born at Aklavik.

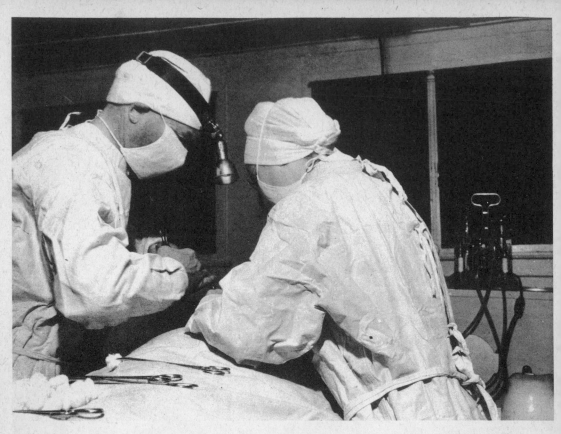

(above) Dr. Livingstone operating at the Anglican Hospital. *(below)* Ferdinand, a bull calf, supplied Aklavik with fresh beef at 50 cents a pound.

Cranberries, reindeer moss, sphagnum and lichens.

Green peas from the garden of the Anglican Mission.

The Livingstones sit down to a roast beef dinner.

Polar Sea Dairy Farm bottle caps.

of the frozen under-earth which provides moisture for the thirsty roots of growing plants. There are no "special" seeds or equipment necessary.

Dr. Livingstone, the only physician and surgeon in this area north of Norman and west of Chesterfield Inlet, is fond of bright-colored clothing. His favorite costume consists of a loud plaid shirt which he insists is the true Livingstone tartan, a striped tie, and a bright yellow sweater. His "parka" is lined in red, and a blue beret or his battered felt hat usually tops off the dazzling picture. The doctor divides his time between the modern Anglican and Catholic hospitals, both of which are electrically lighted, equipped with operating and dental rooms, x-ray equipment and isolation

Ice is cut in winter and stored up to use for drinking water. Any cellar deep enough to utilize the chill of the permanently frozen sub-soil, is an ideal cold storage house, requiring no additional ice.

wards. Each hospital has an iron lung, neither of which has as yet been used. The doctor also makes long journeys both winter and summer to aid people who are unable to travel to the hospitals.

Mrs. Livingstone, who was once her husband's secretary, has the "green thumbs" in the family. She has successfully raised in her truck garden potatoes, cabbage, cauliflower, kale, broccoli, lettuce, radishes, turnips, beets and other vegetables. She even manages to find time to care for several flower beds whose blossoms provide attractive decoration for the house. She also is one of the most active members of the local Red Cross chapter.

As in many a small town the world over the white women of the town gather every Monday at each other's houses for a knitting and crocheting bee,

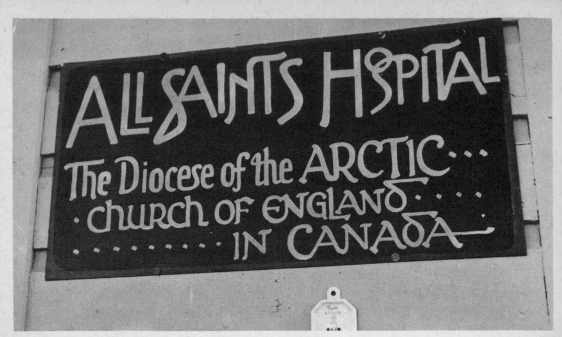

From the Anglican Hospital of Aklavik.

making numerous squares which will eventually be joined to make a complete afghan. When finished it is auctioned or raffled off and the proceeds donated to the Red Cross. On the first Monday of each month the meetings are held in the class room of the Anglican school, and Eskimo and Indian women are invited, and soon learn to master the intricacies of single and double crochet, and knit one purl one.

Like all the schools in the Northwest Territories, those at Aklavik are subsidized by the Government but run by the Missions. Both the Church of England in Canada and the Roman Catholic Church maintain boarding schools for native children which accommodate about 180 pupils, in addition to day schools for the town children. The Eskimo and Indian children attend school for about four or five years, living in dormitories throughout that period. Some of them come great distances to join the class, one student even from a thousand miles away.

The Anglican Church, a white clapboard structure, is the most imposing building in town. At its Mission the native children become Boy Scouts and Girl Guides, drilling in uniform like thousands of other Canadian children in more southerly climes. Strangely enough, a woman's missionary society here solicits funds from the natives for missions in Africa and China, and both Catholic and Anglican churches take up collections in furs.

Aklavik has a post office, four trading posts and two hotels. The latter cater to the business folk who fly in during the winter and the tourists who come in summer. The tourists bathe in Arctic waters and take side trips to nearby towns and to the edge of the Polar Sea.

In spring, green things push and pierce their way quickly through the earth, while high above birds paint the sky with their colors and fill the air with their songs. Red-winged blackbirds, robins, whiskey-jacks, golden plovers, exquisite white swans, ducks and geese are all to be seen here. Croaking black ravens, too, and the familiar Arctic tern, which migrates halfway round the world from the Arctic to the Antarctic each year.

What of the future of this little Arctic town of Aklavik? Will it remain merely an important fur trading center sending out almost a million dollars worth of fur each year as it did in 1943? Will its future be linked with regular flights across the Polar Sea as great in length as the yearly migration of the little grey tern? Will it become one of Canada's ports of entry? Will it be the last port of call for a fleet of freighting submarines making their weekly trip to Siberia, Murmansk or some Scandinavian port? The next decade or two will tell the story!

The glimpse you have had of Arctic life in six Polar communities is a preview of things to come. If not we, then certainly our children will live to see vast portions of this once useless country populated, industrialized and prosperous. Here is our new frontier.

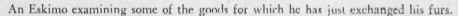

An Eskimo examining some of the goods for which he has just exchanged his furs.

INDEX

A

Aklavik 7, 130, 133-155; Anglican Mission 154; aviation 134; dairy farming 145-153; reindeer meat at, 138; river freighting 142-144; Roman Catholic Mission 146, 154; vegetation 134, 146-53.
Alaska 3, 101-128; aviation 104-105; transportation 104.
Alaska (Alcan) Highway 130.
Aleutian Islands 102, 104.
Amundsen, Roald 107.
Anchorage 102.
Angmagssalik 14.
Arctic Institute of Leningrad 76, 80.
Arctic Ocean, see Polar Sea.
Attu Island 104.
Aurora borealis 138.
Aviation 1; in Alaska 104; in Canadian Arctic 130, 132; future routes 2, 132; use of, in ice reporting 75-76.

B

Baffin Bay 26, 30.
Baffin Island 24, 129.
Bahr, Andrew 138.
Baltic Sea 66.
Banks Island 129, 139.
Banks Islanders 139-140.
Barges on Mackenzie River 142-144.
Bear's Island 92.
Beaufort Sea 138.
Bell, J. Macintosh 132.
Bering Sea 74.
Bering Strait 75.
Bjarney (Bear Island) 22; see also Disko Island.
Blosseville Coast 10.
Borden Island 129.
Bristol Bay 105.
Brooks Range 104.
Brower, Charles D. 107.
Buckner, Simon B. 104.

C

Cabot, John 130.
Camsell, Charles 132.
Canadian Arctic 3, 129-155; aviation 130; minerals 130; reindeer station 138; weather and radio stations 134.
Canadian Pacific Airlines 136.
Cape Farewell 10, 12.
Caribou 29, 119, 138; see also reindeer.
Cryolite 15.

D

Danish Arctic Station 32-37.
Davis, John 12.
Daylight and darkness in Arctic Regions 137-138.
de Kauffmann, Henrik 15.
Demarcation Point 104.
Dickens, "Punch" 134.
Disko Bay 26.
Disko Fjord 26.
Disko Island (Kekertarssuak) 7, 14, 21-37; size and shape 24-25; springs 26; vegetation 22, 34-37; see also Bjarney.
Dutch Harbor 102.

E

East Siberian Sea 76.
Echo Bay 132.
Edmonton 136.
Egede, Hans 12.
Elisofon, Eliot 145.
Ellesmere Island 10, 129.
Ellsworth, Lincoln 107.
Erik the Red 10.
Eskimos 4; "civilization's" effect on 102; first settlers of Alaska 101-102; Greenland 12; legend of Disko Island 21-22; mechanical skill 134-136; Point Hope 120-122; whaling beliefs 120-122.
Explorers Club 137.

F

Fairbanks 102, 105, 118, 128, 130, 136.
Finnie, Richard 130, 134, 146.
Fiske, Willard 38-39; as patron of Grimsey 45-46.
Flagstoneland, see Helluland.
Forestland, see Markland.
Fort Norman Oil Wells 130, 136.
Fort Yukon 94, 104, 105.
Foxe Basin 129.

Franz Josef Land 80.
Frobisher, Martin 12.
Frozen sub-soil (permafrost) 89-90; 146.

G

Gällivare 61, 64, 65, 70, 71; iron mines 62.
Giddings, Louis 109, 110-111.
Godhavn (Lievely) 30, 31; dwellings 30;
   Danish Arctic Station at, 32-37.
Godthaab 14, 22.
Great Bear Lake 130; radium found at,
   130-132.
Greenland 2, 3, 4, 44; American relations
   15; coal 29-30; cryolite 15; discovery and
   colonization 10-12; holidays 32; medicine
   14; republic 9, 12; size 9, 10; trade 12, 14;
   vegetation 10.
Grimsey 38-51; animal life 42-43; chess 38-
   39, 45; cooperatives 48; egg-gathering 42;
   farms 46, 47; housing 50; schooling 48-
   49; sea birds 40-42; sheep 46-47.
Gruber, Ruth 92.
Gunnbjörn 10.

H

Helluland (Flagstoneland) 22, 24.
Housing in Disko Island 30; in Grimsey
   50; in Igarka 89-90.
Hudson Bay 2.
Hudson, Henry 12.
Hudson Land 12.
Hudson's Bay Company 140.

I

Ice-breaker 76, 88-89.
Ice cap, see Inland Ice.
Ice pack 4.
Ice reporting 75-76.
Icebergs 4, 21, 30.
Iceland 4, 10, 24, 44, 137; cooperatives 48;
   literacy in, 40; parliament 40; reading in,
   40; Arctic portion of, 40.
Igarka 7, 76, 86-99; agricultural experiment
   station 92-96; growing season 94; hous-
   ing 89-90; lumbering 88-89; planning of,
   87-88; Polar Theatre at, 96-97; rapid
   growth 87; shipping 88-89.
Indians 101, 102.
Inland Ice 9, 10.
Institute for the Peoples of the North 82.

Ipiutak 108-120; artifacts 118, 119; graves
   118; houses 118; National Monument
   128; people 119; diet of, people 119; prehistoric burials 108-109.
Ivigtut 14-15.

J

Jabbertown 110.
Julianehaab District 10.

K

Kara Sea 88, 89.
Karlsefni, see Thorfinn Karlsefni.
Kekertarssuak (The Big Island) 24; see
   Disko Island.
Khrenikova, Marie M. 94.
King William Island 129.
Kingiktorsuak Island 24.
Kiruna 61, iron ore 71; mine 62, 71-73;
   planned by Hjalmar Lundbohm 66.
Kirunavaara (Kiruna Mountain) 61, 66, 71.
Kiska Island 104.
Kola Peninsula 75, 82.
Kotzebue 128.
Kulaks 91.
Kutdlisat 29-30.

L

La Bine, Gilbert 130.
Lapland 3, 53-60. See also Swedish Lapland.
Lapps 53-60.
Larsen, Helge 109, 119, 128.
Leif Eriksson 12, 22.
Lena River 76.
Levanevsky, Sigismund 136.
Lievely, see Godhavn.
Lindbergh, Charles and Anne 133, 134.
Livingstone, Leslie David 145-153.
Livingstone, Mrs. Leslie 153.
Lulea 66.
Lulea River 62.
Lundbohm, Hjalmar 66.
Luossavaara 61, 66, 71.

M

Mackenzie River 133, 134, 145; barges on,
   142-144.
Mackenzie River 141.
Maktak 32.
Malmberget 61, 70.

Maps, Mercator projection 2; northern hemisphere, 2-3.
Markland (Forestland) 22, 24.
Melville Island 129.
Meteorites 30.
Meteorological stations, in Canadian Arctic 134; in Soviet Arctic 75.
Moonlight in Arctic Regions 137-138.

N

Nalukataktut 126-128.
Nansen, Fridtjof 12.
Narwhal 26.
Narvik 62, 66.
Nobile, Umberto 107.
Nome 105, 128.
Nordenskjöld, A. E. 30.
Nordvyk 76.
Norman Oil Wells, see Fort Norman Oil Wells.
Northeast Land 4.
Northeast Passage 75.
Northern Sea Route Administration 75, 92.
Northwest Passage 130.
Nugsuak Peninsula 22.

O

Oimekon, cold pole of world 82.
Ostroumova, Valentina P. 92.

P

Papanin Expedition 4.
Peary Land 10.
Peary, Robert E. 12, 30.
Peffer, Henry 145.
Peffer's Trading Post 140, 145.
Permafrost, see Frozen sub-soil.
Polar Sea Dairy Farm 145-154.
Point Barrow 104, 105-107.
Point Hope (Tigerak) 105, 108-128; reindeer 128; whaling 119-126; see also Ipiutak.
Polar Sea 3-4; animal life 4; Wilkins flights over 137-138.
Polar Stations in Soviet Arctic 75; 80-82.
Porjus Falls 62.
Porjus Hydroelectric Plan 62-64, 73.
Porsild, Erling 34.
Porsild, Morten Pedersen 21, 32-33, 34, 37.
Porsild, Thorbjörn 34.

Port Radium 130.
Prince Patrick Island 129.

R

Radium, discovery of, at Great Bear Lake 130-132.
Railroad in Swedish Lapland 65, 66, 72-73.
Rainey, Froelich B. 109, 118, 119, 122, 128.
Rasmussen, Knud 13, 30, 109.
Red River 30.
Reindeer 53-54, 73, 102, 128; meat 138; station 138; see also Caribou.
Richards Island Reindeer Station 138.
Ross, John 30.
Rudolf Island 80.

S

Savssat 26-27.
Schmidt, Otto J. 80.
Schools in Iceland 48-49; in Northwest Territories 154; in Swedish Lapland 66-69.
Seals 44.
Sheep in Greenland 15; on Grimsey 46-47.
Shefferus, Johannes 64.
Siberia 4; early history 74-75; forests 88; furs 74-75; see also Soviet Arctic.
Snorri Thorfinnsson 23.
Somerset Island 129.
Soviet Arctic 3, 74-99; industrialization 80; native peoples 74, 82; polar stations 75, 80-82.
Spitsbergen 3, 4, 44.
Stalin, Josef 87.
Steenstrup, K. J. V. 30.
Stefansson, Vilhjalmur 3, 80, 107, 139.
Swedish Lapland 61-73; electricity in, 61-62; mineral deposits 64-69; railroad 65, 66, 72-73; water power 62.

T

Taimyr Peninsula 82.
Thomas process 65, 66.
Thorfinn Karlsefni 22.
Tigerak, see Point Hope.
Torne River 65.

V

Vaigat 26.
Verkhoyansk 82.
Victoria Island 129.
Vinland (Wineland) 12, 22, 24.

W

Whale, blue 120; bowhead 119, 120, 124-126; hunting beliefs of Eskimos 120-121; white 26, 29, 44.
Whaling 31-32; at Point Hope 119-126.
Whitehorse 130.
Wilkins, Hubert 107; flights over Polar Sea 137-138; search for Levanevsky 136-138.
Women's role in Soviet Arctic 92.
World distribution of land 2; of people 2.
Wrangel Island 1.
Wright, Orville and Wilbur 1.

Y

Yenisei River 86, 88.

160